Praise for *The* .... *Focused Guide to Leadership*

II Wow, a great accumulation of downright common sense packed into an easy to read and even easier to implement book about recognising and playing to your strengths, to get the best possible outcome in your professional life. The fast route to top performance. Highly recommended.

SIMON CULMER, MANAGING DIRECTOR UK & IRELAND, AVAYA

II Strengths-focused leadership has transformed how my team works. This book brilliantly sets out the roadmap to game change team performance. Essential reading for anyone looking to inspire their team to reach new heights and be happier!

JERRY CLOUGH, CHIEF OPERATING OFFICER, NORTHERN, EASTERN AND WESTERN DEVON CLINICAL COMMISSIONING GROUP

II This book is a goldmine for readers who want to be the leaders they have the potential to be. It is bursting with useful content: frameworks, case studies, activities, references and resources. I can see the potential of this for individual development, for coaching scenarios and in team situations. This book has a spirit of hope, potential and possibility. As leaders, we all need some of that.

DR HELEN BEVAN, CHIEF TRANSFORMATION OFFICER, NHS IMPROVING QUALITY

II This is a coaching guide in your pocket – Kathy and Mike's considerable experience is distilled into practical steps to release the untapped potential that exists in every individual. Use it if you want to develop a more empowered and energised organisation.

ANNE WILSON, REGIONAL INNOVATION AND LEARNING DIRECTOR

II A box full of tools that will revolutionise your leadership style.

NOAMAN HASAN, HEAD OF GLOBAL CHANGE DELIVERY, ASIA PACIFIC REGION, HSBC

" This book is an invaluable resource for anyone who wants to lead by bringing out the best in people and building great teams that deliver.

DR MARTIN MCSHANE BSC MS MRCGP MA, DIRECTOR FOR IMPROVING THE QUALITY OF LIFE FOR PEOPLE WITH LONG TERM CONDITIONS, NHS ENGLAND

" A step-by-step guide that converts our new understanding of strengths into practical activities that every leader can apply to develop themselves and their teams.

DR CARMELINA LAWTON SMITH, SENIOR LECTURER, INTERNATIONAL CENTRE FOR COACHING AND LEADERSHIP DEVELOPMENT, OXFORD BROOKES UNIVERSITY BUSINESS SCHOOL

" A compelling, practical guide to getting the most out of yourself and your people.

HELEN SHUTE, HEAD OF MARKETING AND SUPPORTER DEVELOPMENT, NATIONAL TRUST

" Very practical, step-by-step guide with easy-to-remember acronyms to help every leader and team maximise their strengths.

BRIAN O. UNDERHILL, Ph.D. EXECUTIVE COACH AND CEO, COACHSOURCE. AUTHOR *EXECUTIVE COACHING FOR RESULTS*

" A brilliant insight into what good management is all about: passion, self-improvement, mentoring and leadership. This book is no dry guide, but a thoughtful, encouraging teacher at your side as you navigate the challenges of modern business.

ROBERT MOORE IS AN AUTHOR AND AWARD-WINNING JOURNALIST. HE IS CURRENTLY WASHINGTON CORRESPONDENT FOR ITV NEWS

The Strengths-Focused Guide to Leadership

The Strengths-Focused Guide to Leadership

Identify your talents and
get the most from your people

Mike Roarty
Kathy Toogood

Harlow, England • London • New York • Boston • San Francisco • Toronto • Sydney
Auckland • Singapore • Hong Kong • Tokyo • Seoul • Taipei • New Delhi
Cape Town • São Paulo • Mexico City • Madrid • Amsterdam • Munich • Paris • Milan

PEARSON EDUCATION LIMITED
Edinburgh Gate
Harlow CM20 2JE
United Kingdom
Tel: +44 (0)1279 623623
Web: www.pearson.com/uk

First published 2014 (print and electronic)

The rights of Mike Roarty and Kathy Toogood to be identified as authors of this work have been asserted by them in accordance with the Copyright, Designs and Patents Act 1988.

Pearson Education is not responsible for the content of third-party internet sites.

ISBN: 978-1-292-06417-8 (print)
       978-1-292-06419-2 (PDF)
       978-1-292-06420-8 (ePub)
       978-1-292-06418-5 (eText)

British Library Cataloguing-in-Publication Data
A catalogue record for the print edition is available from the British Library

Library of Congress Cataloging-in-Publication Data
Roarty, Mike.
  The strengths-focused guide to leadership : identify your talents and get the most from your team /
  Mike Roarty, Kathy Toogood. -- First Edition.
       pages cm
  Includes bibliographical references and index.
  ISBN 978-1-292-06417-8 (Print) -- ISBN 978-1-292-06419-2 (PDF) -- ISBN 978-1-292-06420-8 (ePub)
  -- ISBN 978-1-292-06418-5 (eText)
  1. Leadership. 2. Strategic planning. 3. Teams in the workplace. I. Toogood, Kathy. II. Title.
  HD57.7.R623 2014
  658.4'092--dc23
                             2014029520

10 9 8 7 6 5 4 3 2 1
18 17 16 15 14

Cover design by Two Associates
Print edition typeset in 9pt Melior by 30
Printed by Ashford Colour Press Ltd, Gosport

NOTE THAT ANY PAGE CROSS REFERENCES REFER TO THE PRINT EDITION

Contents

About the authors

Mike Roarty is an executive and team coach, leadership trainer and consultant. With Kathy Toogood he is a Director of Strengths Focused Leadership Ltd, a company specialising in bringing this style of leadership to large organisations. He is also Director of People Potential and Performance Ltd.

Mike has held national strategic responsibility for people development in previous roles. His work with leadership teams in the NHS, the world's fourth largest organisation, gives him a firm understanding of complex systems and the importance of cultural change in achieving large-scale transformation. He has also held creative and management roles in the music business, which bring a particular creativity to his work.

With 15 years of supporting leaders and teams to achieve stronger results through developing solution-focused and strengths-focused approaches, Mike now works regularly on organisational development programmes built around a strengths-focused culture.

Mike's clients have spanned a range of sectors: pharmaceuticals, banking, IT, retail, music business, local authorities, NHS, social care and voluntary sectors.

Mike has a Masters degree in Coaching and Neuro Linguistic Programming from Kingston University, and is a Chartered Member of the Chartered Institute for Personnel and Development. He lives in Buckinghamshire with his wife and son.

Kathy Toogood is an executive coach, trainer and facilitator and is co-Director of Strengths Focused Leadership Ltd. Kathy is also Director of Clearly Inspired Ltd. The purpose of both these organisations is to support leaders in maximising their own effectiveness and that of their teams in order to deliver tangible benefits to their business outcomes.

Kathy spent 13 years as a personnel and training professional within the retailing sector before moving on to an independent coaching, training and consulting role. Kathy's projects range from working one-to-one with executives to partnering with clients to design, deliver and manage bespoke leadership and team development programmes, always bringing the strengths-focused principles to her work. Kathy has worked with a wide range of large organisations spanning finance, pharmaceuticals, manufacturing, retail, utilities, service industries, management consultancies, airline services, local and regional government and the NHS.

Kathy has a Masters degree in Coaching and Mentoring Practice from Oxford Brookes University. She lives in Bedfordshire with her husband and two children.

For more information visit:

www.sfleadership.co.uk
www.coach-ppp.co.uk
www.clearlyinspired.co.uk

Acknowledgements

The ideas and tools described in this book have grown from many years of interactions with our clients. Leaders, managers, teams, departments, organisations, customers, patients – all of these have challenged and refined our thinking along the way. Our huge thanks to them all.

In the course of writing the book a number of people have given valuable feedback and helped shape the final version: Charlie Shaw, Clare Burgum, David Russell, Mark McKergow, Nicole Hay-Carter, Roland Howard, Sophie Bizeuil (as well as very valuable coaching), and Sandra Henson.

We also want to thank Jerry Clough, Chief Operating Officer of NEW Devon CCG, who gave us a wonderful opportunity to help develop a strengths-focused organisation in the western locality of the country's largest clinical commissioning group. We also appreciate the opportunity given to us by Alina Sandell, Head of Talent and Transformation at Veolia UK, to work with her on embedding a strengths focus in their talent management processes.

At FT Publishing we have valued the professional and perceptive support of Nicole Eggleton, Senior Commissioning Editor, and we thank Terry Clague for introducing us to Pearson.

Finally our thanks go to our partners and families for all the exceptional support and encouragement throughout – to Jill, Dominic and Casey (Mike); and to David, Joe, Annabel, Helen, Katie and Charlie (Kathy).

Introduction

I'll go anywhere as long as it's forward.
David Livingstone, explorer

SO YOU ARE IN A LEADERSHIP ROLE. What do you want to get from it?

'Well, that's easy,' you may be saying. 'I want to be successful.' Yes, of course. And how you define 'successful' might be very individual. If you work in a bank, or in a university, or in a hospital, or run your own business, your definition of success may be shaped by that environment. And it may or may not have a financial measurement.

You may also add, 'And I want to enjoy my work.' That's great news, because in our experience, not every leader we've coached makes that point early on. Unfortunately some people assume that work won't be enjoyable. Hard to believe – but true.

Some people add a third point. 'I want to be doing something that I am good at,' they say. Good point, you may think, but isn't that the same as the first point about being successful? On first appearance it may look that way, but once again our experience of coaching leaders tells us that these two points are not the same. You can be good at something that doesn't deliver you or your organisation success or good results. You can also be getting great results for your organisation and feeling that you are not getting the opportunity to use your best skills or strengths. That situation won't satisfy you in the long term.

Real success for you as a leader is about being at the intersection of these three circles:

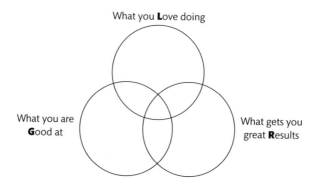

Success = L+G+R. This model is based on one originally devised to describe successful companies.[1] It works equally well as a model for successful leaders. Our quote from the famous explorer David Livingstone implies that you'll want to know that our tools and techniques in this book will work. If the model makes sense to you then strengths-focused leadership will make sense to you because the model is also a description of what strengths-focused leaders do, and what they encourage those they lead to do. Therein lies real success. This book is the practical 'how to' of making it happen.

Why read this book?

As we've just said, this is a 'how to' book. Each chapter begins by clarifying the outcomes you can expect to get from reading it, and these outcomes are a practical mixture of:

▌ key ideas;

▌ real-time exercises to do as you work your way through the book;

▌ straightforward guidelines for implementing back at work in your role as a leader.

It's not a book that you will read and think 'that's interesting' and put aside. It's a living toolkit to changing the way you think and behave for the better.

It will show you how, as a leader, you are likely to be the best leader you can be if you play to your strengths. If you've been a leader for a while

---

1 Collins, J. (2001) *Good to Great: Why some companies make the leap... and others don't*, London, Random House.

you may feel that you already know what your strengths are. You may have been through 360 degree feedback a number of times and be clear about what sorts of things you are good at. Great! This book invites you to stretch your thinking a little further on that. Which of the strengths that you may have identified in 360 degree feedback, or in other ways, are the ones that really inspire and motivate you, and which of them don't? From talking to many people in leadership roles, or in any role, we find that some of the things that people are good at they also love to do, and some of them they don't.

This book will clarify where you can add most value and energise yourself, your team and your organisation by being clear where your strengths, by our definition, lie and how you can make more of them.

We'll explain where the idea of focusing on strengths came from, how it connects to other approaches, and the evidence that suggests it is worth giving it a go.

At its root, a strengths focus is about a way of thinking – a mindset. This book will clarify exactly what the key principles of that mindset are. As well as that, our model of strengths-focused leadership will show you how to incorporate that mindset into the day-to-day activity of leading a team or an organisation. We'll clarify how you can take that strengths-focused mindset into one-to-one conversations, team meetings, coaching conversations, and even into employee processes such as recruitment, performance management and development planning.

Many of the leaders with whom we have worked have led teams that were feeling stressed and demotivated. They saw this as part of a less than ideal culture in the team. Of course, a key player in the culture of a team is the leader. So one of the tools at the disposal of a strengths-focused leader is the opportunity to create a strengths-focused team culture. In a team that regularly focuses on what is working, there is the energy to then focus on building more of that. And as Dewitt Jones, the world-famous photographer and leadership speaker tells us, '*By celebrating what's right . . . we find the energy to fix what's wrong.*'[2] This book will show a leader how to interact with people on a day-to-day basis in a way that builds a strengths-focused culture where people flourish.

---

2 Jones, D. (2001) 'Celebrate What's Right With the World', available at www.celebratewhatsright.com Accessed 21.7.14.

What about weaknesses? You, like everyone else, have them. The people that you lead have them. In fact, on some occasions using one of your strengths too much may actually be a weakness! For you and for each of those individuals that you lead, your weaknesses may or may not be relevant to the goals you each need to achieve. In some situations they probably will be and in some they won't. This book will explain how to approach weaknesses from a position of strength. We have already mentioned the idea of focusing on what we are good at to find the energy to 'fix' what we are not good at. However, there are a number of different approaches to working with an individual weakness that we will explain – it will be about finding the right tool for the right situation. The strengths focus does not ignore weaknesses – what it does is give you a different way to approach them that brings maximum energy to working with them in a constructive results-focused way.

If you are a professional coach, mentor or consultant your interest in the book may be how to be more strengths-focused in your work with leaders. We are confident this book will offer you a range of tools to apply to your work. If you are an HR or OD professional, keen to find out how to develop a strengths-focused organisation, this book should offer you a sequence of useful steps to pilot in your organisation.

We believe that strengths-focused leadership will help you to feel that you are making a real difference – not just to the results that your people get, but to their quality of life, and their own personal growth and fulfilment. What if they were to say in the future, 'That was the best team I was ever in', or 'That organisation means so much to me'? If that interests you, read on.

What's in the book?

To address the points we have just outlined here is how we have structured the book.

We have organised it into three main parts:

Part 1 presents you with the main ideas and concepts that underpin a focus on strengths. It presents you with the key headlines from the most recent research that demonstrate the value and benefits of focusing on strengths. It also clarifies the mindset of a strengths-focused leader, and introduces our **MORE** model, which gives you four straightforward steps to strengths-focused leadership.

Part 2 explores our **MORE** model in depth. The first step is about identifying and developing your own strengths (the '**M**y strengths' element) and the second is about supporting **O**thers you lead to do the same. The third step is then about building a strengths focus into your **R**egular day-to-day conversations. The fourth and final step is about embedding the approach into **E**mployee processes (performance appraisal, development planning and recruitment). This part of the book has been particularly shaped by our real experiences of helping leaders, teams and organisations to develop a strengths-focused culture.

Part 3 looks at other business challenges where you can gainfully employ strengths-focused leadership, such as building high-performing teams, leading change and developing strategy.

Throughout the book you will find a practical 'how to' focus. We involve you in exercises, we present you with real examples and we offer you tools you can begin applying in your work immediately.

All of this has come from our own real experience over the last 10 years of working with leaders, their teams and organisations as a whole. It's what works. We're sure it will work for you, and this book shows you the practicalities of how to do it.

How to read this book

The book follows a sequential structure, with each chapter building on previous ones, particularly with the four steps of our **MORE** model. However, you may want to dip in and out according to what takes your interest. To help you with this we will refer you to anything in the previous chapters of the book that may be particularly relevant to the one you are reading.

It's also worth mentioning that the book, through its exercises, gives you time away from the 'doing' of your work, for reflection. Leaders tell us that this active reflection is extremely useful and leads to more considered and effective action.

We want you to interact with this book as much as possible; where you see the notepad icon:

grab a pad or your tablet and make notes as you go along.

Action points

At the end of each of the chapters (except Chapter 1) we summarise the action points coming out of that chapter. This will help you focus and embed the learning from the chapter into your behaviour and actions back at work. We summarise all the action points in the section towards the end of the book called 'Putting it all together'. You could use this as your development plan to put all the elements of the book into action, or the particular ones you want to focus on.

Our website

Our book is also backed up with online resources that you can access. These include downloads of forms and tools, and video clips showing how some of the key tools are used. You can download all the exercises and templates from our website, either in one file, or as individual exercises. In the text you'll see this symbol:

when there is a downloadable resource. You'll find these at www.sfleadership.co.uk.

Other websites

We also refer you to other websites and resources to build on what you learn from the book. Some of these are online strengths assessments. One of the great benefits of this book is that we are not using it to sell one particular online tool. So we present the pros and cons of the various online assessment tools. And importantly, you don't need to use any of them. We show you how to identify and develop your strengths using our 5 Step Strengths Map and R5 Action Plan. There is no extra fee for this – it's all within the book and our free downloadable resources.

If you have any questions, comments or feedback, email us on info@sfleadership.co.uk.

part

What is strengths-focused leadership?

Part 1 of this book introduces you to the underlying principles of strengths-focused leadership and what that means.

Before you can begin to adopt a strengths focus it is important that you are really clear about what we mean by a strength, so that is where we will start. It is also important that you understand why you may want to adopt more of a strengths focus in the way you lead yourself and others and are clear about the benefits that it can bring to you and your team. For some, it is also important to know the history and empirical evidence that underpins the strengths approach.

We have already had positive feedback about the practical nature of the content of the book, but before we share with you the many strengths-focused tools and techniques for you to apply in your leadership, it is important that you understand what the mindset of a strengths-focused leader is. You may want to check whether you already have a strengths-focused mindset, or you may want to know how you can develop this further. Subscribing to the beliefs of a strengths-focused leader is fundamental to you being able to implement some of the most effective people management techniques that you might ever have come across in your management career.

With our aim being to make this book as practical as possible, in Part 1 we will introduce you to the **MORE** model for strengths-focused leadership. We will explain the model and later expand on it in depth in Part 2.

In summary, this is what we will cover in Part 1:

1. What is strengths-focused leadership all about and why is it relevant to you?

2. What mindset and beliefs does a strengths-focused leader hold?

What is a strengths focus and why is it important?

And the only way to do great work is to love what you do
Steve Jobs, entrepreneur and CEO of Apple Inc.

A STRENGTHS-FOCUSED LEADER is one who seeks greater results by ensuring that they and the people they lead are able to play to their strengths. And what do we mean by playing to our strengths? This expression has been around for many years, but when we talk about 'strengths', what exactly is a strength? And where do weaknesses fit in?

In the field of Positive Psychology and in research on successful businesses and organisations there is a growing body of evidence to support a strengths focus, revealing many benefits to individuals, teams and organisations. In this chapter we will clarify the evidence that underpins strengths-focused leadership.

Playing to your strengths may not be a new idea, but since its appearance in psychology around 40 years ago, interest in the impact of adopting a strengths focus has been building rapidly. Increasingly, leaders are realising that taking a strengths focus is a fast route to enabling themselves and their teams to flourish.

By the end of this chapter, you will have answers to the following questions:

1. What is a 'strength'?
2. Where do weaknesses fit into the strengths picture?
3. What are the benefits of focusing on strengths?

4   What is the evidence behind strengths-focused leadership?

5   To what else is a strengths focus connected?

What is a 'strength'?

People might be forgiven for making the assumption that when we talk about a person's strengths, we are talking *only* about what they are good at. However, being good at something is only half of the strengths picture. Consider this: you might be very good at something, but hate doing it. To give you an example, I (Kathy) am very good at checking detail when I have to, but I find detailed work such as doing my VAT return boring and tedious even though I can do it very well. It is therefore not a strength of mine.

What really defines a person's strength is whether they are good at an activity *and* get good results in it, *and* they love doing it because they get *energised and motivated* by doing it.

When you really play to your strengths, you feel motivated and energised. You feel like you are being authentic or true to yourself and, as a result, good performance is likely to follow. Strengths are an intrinsic part of who you are, a means to performing at your best and a key to living a fulfilling and rewarding life.

We offer this simple and useful definition of a strength:

> A strength is something that you are good at, that energises and motivates you and gives you great results.

We will now break that down and look at each of the elements of that definition.

▌ **A strength is something that you are good at.** If you are energised and drawn to activities that allow you to use your strengths, you will feel like you are performing at your very best. Playing to your strengths definitely contributes to good performance, and you are likely to become very good at the particular activities which utilise your strengths. The very act of practising certain behaviours will inevitably lead to better performance in them.

Whether or not something is a strength is also context-dependent. A strength applied in the wrong place or in the wrong amount might be perceived as a weakness in the eyes of others.

▌**A strength is something that energises and motivates you.** As well as identifying things you are good at, another way of identifying your strengths is to think about those things that you love doing and that energise and motivate you. When you use your strengths you might talk about 'feeling in my element' or 'in the flow'. The state of 'flow'[1] happens when you are engaged in an activity that you love, such that you can lose all sense of time and you inevitably find that are doing your best work.

▌**A strength is something that gives you good results.** If you are engaged in tasks which you are good at and that energise and motivate you, it probably goes without saying that this will lead to great results. You will probably know yourself when you are delivering outstanding results, but if in doubt this could be confirmed by others.

So it's by playing to your strengths that you will find you deliver some outstanding results.

Exercise: Exploring your strengths

This is an exercise for you to do with someone else, the purpose of which is to begin to think about what some of your strengths might be.

1 Find someone to do this exercise with and each take a few minutes to write down a couple of things that you are good at, that you love to do and that really energise and motivate you. Also write down a couple of things that you're not good at, that you hate doing and that really drain you.

2 Take it in turns to tell each other about the things you are good at and love doing. Then take it in turns to tell each other about the things you are not good at and that drain you.

3 What did you notice about each other when you were talking about the things you love doing, compared to talking about the things you don't? What did you each notice about the impact on yourself when talking about these things?

---

1 Csikszentmihalyi, M. (1990) *Flow: The psychology of optimal experience*, New York, Harper & Row.

If you have done this exercise, we are sure that by now you have a good understanding of what a strength is and how important it is that you consider a strength to be not just something you are good at, but also something that you love doing and that energises and motivates you. We are sure that you have also noticed how energising it is to talk about what you love doing, and how draining it can be to focus on what you are not good at.

Some people observe that strengths sound very similar to values or those things that are important to you. We would agree with that and our view is that strengths are really values in action!

Summary

Playing to your strengths builds on an awareness of what you love doing and what energises you. It involves you consciously finding ways of applying your strengths to what you are doing, not only in order to lead to higher levels of performance, but also to achieve higher levels of fulfilment and satisfaction in what you are doing.

Where do weaknesses fit into the strengths picture?

You might make the mistake of thinking that strengths-focused leadership means ignoring weaknesses. It would of course be naïve to ignore weaknesses, particularly where they are significantly standing in the way of peak performance. However, with a strengths-focused approach, there are ways of addressing weaknesses that conventional wisdom might not have taken into account.

In contrast to our definition of a strength, we define a weakness in this way:

> A weakness is something that you are not good at, that de-energises and de-motivates you and which tends to lead to poor results.

There is an inherent obsession in the workplace with focusing on what is wrong with people; people tend to have a negativity bias[2] within them. You will undoubtedly be used to seeing individuals and leaders focus on weaknesses and put more energy into fixing what is wrong and filling the

---

2 Rozin, P. and Royzman, E. B. (2001) 'Negativity Bias, Negativity Dominance, and Contagion', *Personality and Social Psychology Review* 5 (4), pp. 296–320.

gaps than into doing more of what is right. Focusing on weaknesses will clearly have a negative impact on people. In fact, focusing on weaknesses leads to less energy, low levels of motivation, poorer performance and, eventually, burn-out. As Albert Einstein said: *'Everybody is a genius. But if you judge a fish by its ability to climb a tree, it will live its whole life believing that it is stupid.'* That's not a good place to be if you are a fish!

So, bearing in mind the potential negative impact of focusing on weaknesses, it is important to ask the question, 'Are the weaknesses relevant or irrelevant?' If they are irrelevant, then you can ignore them. Why invest energy in fixing something that isn't going to be needed? If they are relevant, then you need to deal with them, and there are various strengths-focused ways of doing this, which we will explore (in Chapters 4 and 8).

What are the benefits of focusing on strengths?

So, what do people find happens when they become aware of their strengths and then play to these strengths? We carried out our own research with coaches who have adopted a strengths approach, exploring their perceptions of the benefits of focusing on strengths within coaching conversations.[3] Combining the results of this research with a thorough review of existing literature and empirical evidence, our view is that knowing and using one's strengths leads to these benefits for people:

▌ Easier and more enjoyable goal achievement.

▌ Improved performance; faster and better results.

▌ More energy for doing what you want to do.

▌ A wider perspective and more clarity about choices.

▌ Increased confidence, self-belief and a stronger sense of identity.

▌ Greater satisfaction, fulfilment and engagement.

Easier and more enjoyable goal achievement

Recent studies have shown that people find the achievement of their goals easier and more enjoyable if they are related to their strengths and

---

3 Toogood, K. (2012) 'Strengthening Coaching: An exploration of the mindset of executive coaches using strengths-based coaching', *International Journal of Evidence Based Coaching & Mentoring* (Special Issue No. 6), pp. 72–87.

draw on their strengths.[4] By offering people a route to achieving their goals that plays to their strengths, you show them a way forward that is aligned with where their energy naturally wants to go.

> ## In the real world . . .
>
> Linden was a Business Analyst within an IT department. Linden's manager was keen to ensure that his team members' goals were linked to their strengths. When Linden identified his strengths, he realised that his love of interaction with others was quite an unusual strength in his department, which began to explain why he sometimes found it challenging working with more introspective colleagues.
>
> Alongside his people focus, he also really enjoyed thinking strategically and problem solving. It was perhaps not a surprise that he was in the role he was; his role provided an interface between end users and the IT development team and his role involved translating customers' needs into practical IT solutions. With the support of his manager, Linden realised that his role and all of his business objectives provided him with an opportunity to use these strengths, which had a very motivating effect on him.
>
> Both Linden and his manager noticed the significant impact of Linden identifying his strengths. Especially evident was the energy and enjoyment that he was now demonstrating. He was now able to cut through previously difficult challenges with apparent ease, all as a result of becoming more aware of how he was applying his strengths.

Improved performance; faster and better results

Linked to the assumption that a strengths focus provides the easiest route to goal achievement, playing to your strengths also has an impact on the speed and quality of results. One leader we worked with likened a strength focus to a 'gardening approach', whereby she would plant seeds where they are going to grow best, i.e. when tasks and objectives are aligned with a person's strengths, they will be executed better and faster.

So why do you get faster and better results? Quite simply, it is the result of the powerful energy that comes from applying your strengths to what you are doing, as opposed to putting all your energy into countering a weakness. This is supported by evidence that in setting and reviewing performance objectives, people develop faster and performance improves faster if they are focused on developing strengths.[5]

---

4   Linley, A. P., et al. (2010) 'Using Signature Strengths in Pursuit of Goals: Effects on goal progress, need satisfaction, and well-being, and implications for coaching psychologists', *International Coaching Psychology Review* 5 (1), pp. 6–15.

5   Corporate Leadership Council (2002) *Performance Management Survey*, Washington, DC.

> **In the real world ...**
>
> Linden's manager was also keen to ensure that his development plan was based on developing strengths. This plan focused on two clear areas that were highly motivating and interesting for Linden: communicating with people/building relationships and strategic thinking.
>
> By finding work-based opportunities to put his strengths to work, Linden was eager to put previous 'good ideas' into immediate action and saw some amazingly fast results. His achievements, such as launching and coordinating monthly team briefings, not only helped him develop his strengths faster, but also contributed to improved results in his other business objectives and helped the team and the business too!

More energy for doing what you want to do

It's easy to notice how, just by talking about strengths, you begin to get energised and, as a result of tapping into your strengths, you automatically find positive energy to take action. When you focus on what you are good at and what you are already doing well, it creates a lot of energy in you that motivates you to move forward more easily and quickly. Indeed, a recent study found that people who used their strengths reported higher levels of vitality.[6]

Getting people to talk about their strengths also leads to a more energising conversation that can help people feel much more resilient, especially in times of change. When there is uncertainty, we often find that helping people connect with their strengths gives them some of the fuel they need to move forward, even when they are not quite sure what forward might look like.

> **In the real world ...**
>
> Mark, a senior manager, was working with a team member who was really stuck on writing a best practice manual. When he got her to articulate her strengths and focus on what would be energising for her about getting on with the writing, she stood up and physically stepped forward as she began to identify and specify the actions she could take. Unsurprisingly, she left the coaching session with a lot more energy and eagerness to return to her writing and get her manual finished!

6 Govindji, R. and Linley, A. (2007) 'Strengths Use, Self-Concordance and Well-Being: Implications for strengths coaching and coaching psychologists', *International Coaching Psychology Review* 2 (2), pp. 143–53.

A wider perspective and more clarity about choices

Talking about strengths puts you in a positive and resourceful state and therefore enables you to access more creativity. As a result of this, you are able to think more broadly about your options and have greater clarity of choice.

I (Kathy) sometimes have clients who are in a state of foggy confusion about what actions to take in situations they find themselves in. By helping people take a step back and focus on what is working, I find that they can immediately begin to feel more positive. By combining this more positive mindset with a focus on the strengths that can be drawn upon, people often find that they become 'unstuck' and begin to see that they have more control and are able to make choices. It's not necessarily about finding the perfect answer to a dilemma, but more about being able to see some possible first steps.

Similarly, sometimes people find themselves stuck in a state of 'poor me'. When they are helped to acknowledge the strengths they have, they develop an internal locus of control and accept more control over their outcomes and actions. Having an internal locus of control can also build a sense of resilience and lead to a reduction in stress levels. Recent research has confirmed this link between a focus on strengths and lower levels of stress.[7]

Increased confidence, self-belief and a stronger sense of identity

When you know your strengths and play to your strengths, this can lead to improvements in your level of confidence, self-esteem, self-belief and sense of identity. Indeed, adopting a strengths approach is a critical part of the recipe for helping people build a stronger sense of self and become more of who they want to be.

This growth in confidence is again linked to the building of positive emotions; talking about strengths creates positive emotions that allow you to feel more confident about where you are heading.[8] It enables you to

---

7 Wood, A., et al. (2011) 'Using Personal and Psychological Strengths Leads to Increases in Well-Being over Time: A longitudinal study and the development of strengths use questionnaire', *Personality and Individual Differences* 50 (1), pp. 15–19.

8 Fredrickson, B. (2001) 'The Role of Positive Emotions in Positive Psychology: The broaden-and-build theory of positive emotions', *American Psychologist* 56 (3), pp. 218–26.

change the inner conversation you have and get comfortable in being able to speak positively about yourself and, in doing so, build a greater sense of self-efficacy. I have even heard the strengths approach described as 'a Red Bull for confidence'!

By understanding your strengths, you can develop a more rounded view of yourself, feel confident about who you are and stay true to your authentic self. This view is supported by studies that have found that people using their strengths reported higher levels of self-confidence and self-esteem.[9]

In the real world . . .

I (Kathy) was coaching Carrie, a senior leader in a public sector organisation. She was beginning to lose her confidence as a member of a small senior management team. Carrie has strengths in Collaboration with others, Creativity and Developing Others, and she also loves to approach everything with a healthy dose of Enthusiasm.

When we met, she and her colleagues were at the start of driving through a very important stage of change in their organisation. Carrie was excited about this but she was getting tired of feeling like she was on a very different wavelength from her senior colleagues, unable to get them to agree to her ideas for how she might engage and lead people through the change. She was beginning to feel unvalued, to lose her confidence and was thinking about the possibility of moving to a different organisation.

By revisiting her strengths, Carrie was able to see that she could bring something unique to the senior team and that it was important to stay true to herself, rather than feel that she had to change to fit in with everyone else. With renewed confidence and belief in her abilities, she was able to approach her colleagues with more determination to help them see the value in her ideas and allow her to play to her strengths and contribute maximum value to the team. She also learnt to value the diverse strengths of her colleagues!

Greater satisfaction, fulfilment and engagement

An emphasis on strengths in the way people are managed can lead to a higher level of fulfilment or satisfaction in your team. When people are

---

9　Linley, A. P., et al. (2010) 'Using Signature Strengths in Pursuit of Goals: Effects on goal progress, need satisfaction, and well-being, and implications for coaching psychologists', *International Coaching Psychology Review* 5 (1), pp. 6–15. Linley, A., Willars, J. and Biswas-Diener, R. (2010) *The Strengths Book: Be confident, be successful, and enjoy better relationships by realising the best in you*, Coventry, CAPP Press. Proctor, C., Maltby, J. and Linley, A. (2009) 'Strengths Use as a Predictor of Well Being and Health-Related Quality of Life', *Journal of Happiness Studies* 12 (1), pp. 153–69.

encouraged to focus on what energises them and what feels authentic, they will also begin to notice that they feel even better about themselves or have a higher level of overall satisfaction. In addition, leaders who adopt a strengths focus with others will often report they, too, feel more satisfied and fulfilled as a result of the conversation or interaction.

In a nutshell, if people are happy in their work, then they will engage more positively with the world around them, which is better for them and for others, and also for driving higher levels of engagement in organisations.

In the real world . . .

Paul, a manager in a property maintenance organisation, was leading a team of people who were all doing the same job within a customer support team. The role of the customer support team was to provide maintenance duties for customers, ranging from routine repairs, to decorating, to simple emergency plumbing. The organisation was focusing on improving employees' levels of engagement at work and there were requests to look at changing the job content of the customer support team members to make it more motivating for them. They thought that those who were good at decorating, for example, should be allowed to focus more on decorating tasks, although that wasn't necessarily going to be the most commercially sensible approach to take.

Rather than change the job content, Paul decided to spend time helping his team members identify and play to their strengths. He helped them explore what it was that they loved doing in their routine work and helped them think about how they could use these strengths for a higher proportion of their working day, approaching their work in their own unique way. The job hadn't changed but they found that team members were gaining more job satisfaction. Interestingly, the strengths that people identified included things like really enjoying taking time to connect with and talk to the customers. Some liked being able to pay attention to detail, some loved being creative. Each person was unique and, as a result of this approach, Paul began to create a much more engaged and even higher performing team.

What is the evidence behind strengths-focused leadership?

If you are the kind of person who learns best by focusing on learning a practical skill and thinking about how to put it to use at work, and aren't so interested in the history of the ideas behind it, feel free to skip this section.

If you are the kind of person who wants the background, and who knows that by having the background you are able to pick up the skill even faster, then read on!

Leadership and organisational success – the role of a strengths focus

Since the early days of business writing on leadership, from around the 1940s until today, there has been a focus on the role of strong leadership in successful organisations. Some of the best-respected writers on the topic identified a focus on strengths as part of that strong leadership.[10] Many of these early works were more theoretical and anecdotal in their nature, and were not really backed up with any kind of evidence.

Over the last twenty years, readers on the topic of leadership and of business success generally have been more demanding. They have asked for evidence to support any new ideas about great leadership. As a result, a number of authors have collected detailed evidence about business success and the part played in it by leadership.[11] Evidence has emerged about the characteristics of companies who succeed, and of those that maintain that success over many years. Researchers also claim to have identified the nature of leadership in companies that succeed, and how it is different in companies that have not managed to maintain success. As the evidence on successful leadership has emerged over the last 10 years or so, we have started to see a growing body of evidence that successful leadership incorporates a focus on strengths, and that this focus leads to higher employee engagement, customer engagement, safety, productivity and profit.[12] So the message is fairly clear: a focus on strengths is a

10 Haldane, B. (1947) 'A Pattern for Executive Placement', *Harvard Business Review* 25 (4a), pp. 652–63. Drucker, P. F. (1967) *The Effective Executive*, London, Heinemann. Peters, T. J. and Waterman, R. H. (1982) *In Search of Excellence: Lessons from America's best-run companies*, New York, Harper & Row.

11 Collins, J. (2001) *Good to Great: Why some companies make the leap . . . and others don't*, London, Random House. Collins, J. (2006) *Good to Great and the Social Sectors: Why business thinking is not the answer*, Boulder, CO, Random House Business Books. Rath, T. and B. Conchie (2008) *Strengths Based Leadership: Great leaders, teams, and why people follow*, New York, Gallup Press. Kouzes, J. M. and Posner, B. Z. (2002) *The Leadership Challenge*, San Francisco, Jossey-Bass. Zenger, J. H. and Folkman, J. (2009) *The Extraordinary Leader: Turning good managers into great leaders*, New York, McGraw-Hill Professional.

12 Corporate Leadership Council (2002) *Performance Management Survey*. Washington, DC. Linley, A. (2008) *Average to A+: Realising strengths in yourself and others*, Coventry, CAPP Press. Rath, T. and Conchie, B. (2008) *Strengths Based Leadership: Great leaders, teams, and why people follow*, New York, Gallup Press. Collins, J. (2001) *Good to Great: Why some companies make the leap . . . and others don't*, London, Random House. Zenger, J. H., et al. (2012) *How to Be Exceptional: Drive leadership success by magnifying your strengths*, New York, McGraw-Hill. Arakawa, D. and Greenberg, M. (2007) 'Optimistic Managers and their Influence on Productivity and Employee Engagement in a Technology Organisation: Implications for coaching psychologists', *International Coaching Psychology Review* 2 (1), March 2007.

critical success factor for companies wanting to excel. Clearly this is even more critical with the current economic climate and the need to drive greater productivity from fewer resources.

What about weaknesses – what is the right balance?

You may be asking, 'What about weaknesses? Surely organisations and their leaders can't just ignore them.' Well, that depends! Very recent research[13] has shown that leaders who focused their own development on building strengths rather than fixing weaknesses developed significantly more than those who focused on fixing weaknesses. However, the research also suggested that if someone had a significant weakness that seriously risked their own performance, or their team's performance, then this should be top of their development plan.

Some writers and researchers also suggest that the most successful organisational change programmes have a balance between focusing on strengths and weaknesses, and that they tend to achieve better results than those that just focus on fixing weaknesses.[14] Later in the book, in a number of our chapters, we look at how you get this balance right between the focus on strength and the focus on weakness.

Summary of the research

The following table is a useful summary of the research on the application of a strengths focus in business.

Positive impacts of strengths-focused leadership

Impact on employee performance
The Corporate Leadership Council studied 19,000 employees across 34 organisations and 19 countries. It found that an emphasis on performance strengths in appraisals was linked to a 36.4% improvement in performance. In contrast, an emphasis on performance weaknesses was linked to a 26.8% decline in performance.[15]

13 Zenger, J. H., et al. (2012). *How to Be Exceptional: Drive leadership success by magnifying your strengths*, New York, McGraw-Hill.

14 Keller, S. and Price, C. (2011). *Beyond Performance: How great organizations build ultimate competitive advantage*, Hoboken, NJ, Wiley.

15 Corporate Leadership Council (2002) *Performance Management Survey*, Washington, DC.

Impact on employee engagement
Rath and Conchie make it clear that the most effective leaders are always investing in strengths – theirs and others. They describe Gallup's analysis of years of research with over one million work teams, which showed that leaders who focus on and invest in strengths increase engagement. They found that a dismal 1 in 11 (9%) staff were engaged when leaders focused on weaknesses, and a much more hopeful 3 in 4 staff (73%) were engaged when leaders focused on strengths. So leaders who invest in strengths increase engagement eightfold in their teams and in their organisations.[16]
Work unit productivity
Harter, Schmidt and Hayes completed a meta-analysis of over 10,000 work units and over 300,000 employees in 51 companies. They found that work units scoring above the median on the question 'I have the opportunity to do what I do best every day' had 38% higher probability of success on productivity measures.[17]
Customer retention
The study of Harter, Schmidt and Hayes just mentioned also showed that work units scoring above the median on the question 'I have the opportunity to do what I do best every day' had 44% higher probability of success on customer loyalty and retention.

Is this good news for all leaders – private and not-for-profit sectors?

At a common-sense level it would appear obvious that if people are doing what they are good at, and enjoy doing, that motivation and therefore results will be higher. Surely these two elements, motivation and results, are what every leader aspires to? As Eisenhower put it, '*Leadership is the art of getting someone else to do something you want done because he wants to do it.*'

Not all leaders and managers work in the private sector. For those of you who work in the not-for-profit sector of the economy, you may be wondering if the ideas described in the chapter so far also apply to you. Have the development of these ideas also happened in the public and voluntary sectors?

---

16 Rath, T. and B. Conchie (2008) *Strengths Based Leadership: Great leaders, teams, and why people follow*, New York, Gallup Press.

17 Harter, J. K., et al. (2002) 'Business-Unit-Level Relationship between Employee Satisfaction, Employee Engagement, and Business Outcomes: A meta-analysis', *Journal of Applied Psychology* 87 (2) (April 2002), pp. 268–79.

The fact that 'not-for-profit' organisations are significantly different from those in the private sector did not escape Jim Collins, the writer of the seminal book on successful organisations *Good to Great*,[18] so much so that he released a separate short book five years later[19] relating his findings to that sector. The principles of success did indeed remain the same, though financial profit was not the measure of success. Still, in the not-for-profit sector, he identified that successful organisations focused on what they were good at, what they had a passion for, and what would deliver the outcomes they sought. In other words they had alignment between their goals and their strengths.

In the area of Health and Social Care over the last few decades, the thinking on best practice has also seen a growing appreciation of the value of a strengths focus. As early as the late 1980s a strengths approach was growing in mental health services.[20] This eventually grew into a concept known as 'Recovery'. Recovery is a term which has evolved in mental health services worldwide since the early 1990s. It's about seeing past people's deficits, weaknesses and illness to their abilities, their aspirations and their possibilities.[21] This focus on strengths has spread further into Social Care internationally[22] and in Public Health as a whole.[23]

To what else is a strengths focus connected?

With new developments in our society we often find the same idea appearing in different places at the same time, as ideas are shared across a variety of situations and contexts. So it is worth mentioning where else the strengths focus ideas have been developed over the last few decades.

1 **Appreciative inquiry.** This approach appeared in the 1980s and has built its popularity from its effectiveness. It suggests that we

---

18 Collins, J. (2007) *Good to Great: Why some companies make the leap . . . and others don't*, London, Random House.

19 Collins, J. (2006) *Good to Great and the Social Sectors: Why business thinking is not the answer*, Boulder, CO, Random House Business Books.

20 Rapp, C. A. (1998) *The Strengths Model: Case management with people suffering from severe and persistent mental illness*, New York and Oxford, Oxford University Press.

21 Repper, J. and Perkins, R. (2003) *Social Inclusion and Recovery: A model for mental health practice*, Edinburgh, Bailliere Tindall.

22 Saleebey, D. (2012) *The Strengths Perspective in Social Work Practice*, London, Pearson Education.

23 NICE (The National Institute for Health & Clinical Excellence) (2007) *Behaviour Change. NICE public health guidance 6*. www.nice.org.uk/guidance/ph6/resources/guidance-behaviour-change-the-principles-for-effective-interventions-pdf. Accessed 21.7.14

can develop teams and organisations more effectively by asking questions such as 'What are we doing well?' and 'How can we make more of this?' rather than asking 'What problems do we have?' and 'What is causing these problems?'[24]

2 **Solution focus.** Beginning around the same time in the world of therapy as Solution Focused Brief Therapy,[25] the Solution Focus is about focusing on what we want (solution), rather than on what we don't want (problem). It also focuses on finding out what already works well for us, and how to build on this. These solution-focused ideas have spread from the world of therapy into management and organisational development as well as coaching.

3 **Positive psychology.** In 1998, Martin Seligman, then the new President of the American Psychological Association, at its annual conference, suggested in his presidential address that it was time for a new era of psychology that also concentrates on what makes people feel happy and fulfilled (as opposed to just what makes them ill or unhappy). This new era did indeed arrive and the movement has come to be known as Positive Psychology, with many university departments around the world now devoted to it, doing research and gathering evidence about what works and what doesn't work in fostering success and excellence, as opposed to failure. Many of these psychologists have been behind the development of online tools to assess people's strengths, and in the development of organisation processes to support a strengths-focused organisational culture.

Note

Whilst this book is based on cutting-edge thinking, it is a practical manual rather than a book of academic theory. For that reason, this section on the history of the strengths approach has been reasonably short. For those who would like to explore the theory further, the footnotes/references are good places to start.

24 Cooperrider, D. L. and Srivastva, S. (1987) 'Appreciative Inquiry in Organizational Life', *Research in Organizational Change and Development* 1, pp. 129–69.

25 De Shazer, S. (1985) *Keys to Solution in Brief Therapy*, New York, Norton.

2

The mindset of a strengths-focused leader

Your living is determined not so much by what life brings to you as by the attitude you bring to life; not so much by what happens to you as by the way your mind looks at what happens.
(Khalil Gibran, artist, poet and writer)

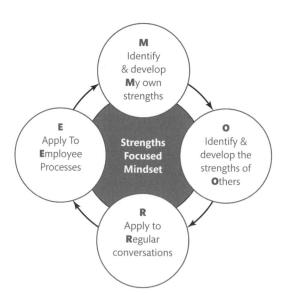

FOR THOUSANDS OF YEARS the greatest thinkers have suggested that the behaviour and achievements of human beings are determined by their thoughts and beliefs. In the last 40 or 50 years psychologists and business writers have analysed the way that successful people think in order to highlight the key ways of thinking that tend to generate better results.

By the end of this chapter you will have answers to the following questions:

1. What is the link between mindset, emotions, behaviour and results?
2. What is the mindset of a strengths-focused leader?
3. How do I develop a strengths-focused mindset?
4. Where can I immediately apply this in my work?

What is the link between mindset, emotions, behaviour and results?

The dictionary definition of 'mindset' is a fixed mental attitude or way of thinking that predetermines a person's responses to and interpretations of situations. The field of psychology tells us that our behaviour is driven by our beliefs, values, and emotions. These behaviours will determine our results. To put things into sequence: we think a certain way about a situation that we are in; this way of thinking about it will dictate how we feel about it – our emotional state; our way of thinking and our feelings about the situation will then strongly influence our behaviour; our behaviour in a situation will then dictate our results. This is captured succinctly in the model that we call the mindset cycle:

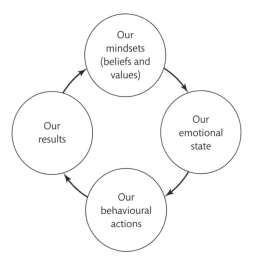

To clarify why this is so important here are two examples:

In the real world . . .

Nigel believes he is not a natural at doing business presentations to groups. The combination of his belief and the feelings of low confidence and high anxiety arising from it leads him to visualise his presentation going badly (forgetting what to say, stumbling over what he does say). All of this creates a dry mouth, sweaty palms, shaky hands and legs, and a hesitant voice as he begins his presentation. He hears himself stutter and this throws his concentration even further and he forgets what he is going to say next. Eventually he stumbles through to the end and receives a muted response, which only goes to confirm his initial view of himself.

Bridget, on the other hand, believes she has a natural touch in getting on with people, and in selling. This strong belief means that she looks forward to her first interaction with a new customer, looking forward to the challenge and confident that she will get a good result. She naturally then gives off a relaxed and confident manner with the new client, with whom she can then confidently build rapport ('I can build rapport with anyone,' she says to herself). So she makes the sale without any great pressure. This is further evidence of her belief in her rapport building and selling skills. Of course it doesn't always result in a sale but, being confident in her abilities, when she doesn't make a sale, she knows that if it's not this customer it will be the next one. And guess what – she's right.

Management literature abounds in examples of how the attitude or mindset that managers have towards themselves and the people they manage affects the results, motivation and even the health of their staff.[1] Here are two more examples to illustrate the point.

In the real world . . .

Tony believes his team are basically lazy. This way of thinking means that Tony feels disappointed, frustrated and sometimes angry when he thinks about them. This then gives rise to critical fault-finding interactions with the team. Since Tony is looking for faults he is likely to find them (whether they are there or not!). This demotivates the team and influences them to underperform. Those faults that Tony inevitably finds, combined with his negative impact on the team in both motivation and performance, leads him then to find

---

1   Arakawa, D. and Greenberg, M. (2007) 'Optimistic Managers and their Influence on Productivity and Employee Engagement in a Technology Organisation: Implications for coaching psychologists', *International Coaching Psychology Review* 2 (1), March 2007. Michie, S. and S. Williams (2003) 'Reducing Work Related Psychological Ill Health and Sickness Absence: A systematic literature review', *Occupational & Environmental Medicine* (60), pp. 3–9.

underperformance and all of this therefore confirms his initial belief about his team. Well at least he was right!

Ayesha believes her team are a talented and capable bunch that will undoubtedly achieve great things with the right encouragement. Ayesha feels energised and enthusiastic in her interactions with them. These enthusiastic interactions with them build their confidence and motivation. She gives them positive feedback about their existing achievements and what she believes they can achieve in the future. Their increased motivation and confidence lead to more energy and productivity and better results, and all of this then reinforces Ayesha's original belief about her team – they're a great team. Right again!

What is the mindset of a strengths-focused leader?

If our way of thinking and our attitudes ultimately affect our results, then there is a mindset behind the strengths-focused leadership approach that generates the results we considered in the evidence mentioned previously (in Chapter 1).

The mindset of a strengths-focused leader

Me

- I am the best leader I can be when I am being authentic and playing to my own strengths.
- As a great leader I don't need to be strong at everything, and others can bring the strengths that I may not have.

Others

- Everyone has strengths that can be harnessed and built on.

Performance

- People perform at their best when expectations are clear and aligned as closely as possible with their strengths.
- People will perform better, be more motivated and engaged and make a stronger contribution if they are enabled to play to their strengths.
- Our strengths are most effective when we use them at the right time, in the right situation, and the right amount. Strengths can be overused and underused.

Developing people

- Helping people identify their strengths helps them use them more.
- People develop faster when I focus on building on their strengths.

Teamwork

▌ Teams can play to their strengths more if they identify one another's strengths.

▌ Aligning the individual strengths in the team to the tasks and goals of the team will increase our success.

Weakness

▌ Celebrating strengths and what is working gives people the energy to address their weaknesses and what is working less well or not working at all.

▌ I view my own and others' weaknesses from a position of strength – looking at how we can use our strengths to address any significant weaknesses.

Our view is that a strengths-focused leader is one who adopts and demonstrates the principles, or mindset, shown in the box above and then exhibits behaviour which is therefore driven by that mindset.

How many of the statements in the box reflect your mindset as a leader? We will examine that question further.

How do I develop a strengths-focused mindset?

Some people are naturally more aware or conscious of their mindset. Others, through training or necessity, have learned to become more aware of it. However, some people may not be very aware of their mindset – they act out behaviours unconscious of the mindset that is driving them.

The following assessment gives you a tool to take stock of your existing mindset. It will help you raise your awareness of the areas of a strengths-focused mindset that you already operate from, and those that you may want to develop more.

Exercise: Assessing your mindset

Think of your last week or two at work and everything that happened during that time. In the following table, in each pair of statements, tick the one that you think most describes your attitude or behaviour during that time.

1. I am pleased with what I was able to accomplish.	☐	☐	1. I didn't manage to achieve very much.
2. I got to do the things that I do best.	☐	☐	2. I did lots of things but I'm not sure which things I'm good at.
3. My team members were a pleasure to work with.	☐	☐	3. My team members were difficult, as they usually are.
4. My team members made excellent contributions.	☐	☐	4. My team members didn't contribute as much as they really should.
5. As far as was possible, the tasks people in the team were occupied with were allocated to them in a way that plays to their strengths.	☐	☐	5. People did the tasks allocated to their role.
6. I gave each and every one of them feedback on their positive contributions.	☐	☐	6. I didn't give much positive feedback. It's not something I do all that much.
7. It was clear to me that people in the team are highly motivated and enjoying their work.	☐	☐	7. Team members didn't look too motivated or enjoying what they were doing. That's the way it usually is.
8. I was able to encourage people to think about where they could perform at an even higher level.	☐	☐	8. I told a few of them what I was not happy about. I do this regularly.
9. I started off our team meeting with a sharing of achievements and successes since our previous meeting.	☐	☐	9. I focused our team meeting on the problems in the team. That's what I usually do.
10. I ended our team meeting looking at what we had achieved during it.	☐	☐	10. I ended our team meeting with a recap on what I need people to do, to ensure the message got through.
11. Where I had to point out weak areas of performance, I communicated my confidence in the person's abilities.	☐	☐	11. Where I had to point out weak areas of performance, I expressed my dissatisfaction.
12. When we addressed a problem I focused the discussion on describing the solution and how we will get there.	☐	☐	12. When we addressed a problem, I ensured we identified the cause and who was responsible.

ASSESSING YOUR SCORE

Count the ticks you made in the left-hand column and then look at which range your score appears in below:

10–12   Congratulations – you're already very strengths focused.

8–10   You lean towards a strengths focus already.

5–7   You're about half way there.

3–5   You lean towards a focus on weakness/deficit.

1–2   Your mindset is very focused on weakness/deficit.

Having assessed your mindset what do you do now if you want to develop a more strengths-focused mindset? Well, if you think back to the mindset cycle, you have four ways of doing it.

1   Your mindset.

When planning your interactions with your team, either one-to-one or with the whole team, take the time to notice what you are telling yourself. What are you assuming to be true about yourself and the team? Reflect on how you can approach those interactions in a way that demonstrates a strengths focus. Look back at 'The mindset of a strengths-focused leader' (page 21). Which principles do you want to demonstrate more of in your next team meeting?

2   Your emotional state.

There are situations where you will want to feel strong and confident. For example, when making an important presentation, at an interview, or when seeking to influence a key stakeholder or customer.

As a leader it is even more important for you to manage your emotional state. This emotional state will impact the emotional state of those you lead, and they will tend to read and be affected by it, regardless of your verbal communication.

The good news is that your emotional state can be directly influenced by what you occupy your mind with as you approach situations. If you occupy yourself with thinking about your weaknesses, you are unlikely to feel strong and confident.

If you occupy your mind with recalling specific memories of (relevant) situations where you have felt strong and confident, the associated emotions, feeling strong and confident, are automatically re-created in you in the present. Every Olympic athlete makes use of this technique as they approach a race or athletic performance.

As a strengths-focused leader you can develop habits which create a strong resourceful state. This involves you reflecting on your work and actions in a strengths-focused way. Ask yourself at the end of each working day: What have I achieved today? What did I do particularly well that I also enjoyed doing? What did my team members do well today? What strengths can we take to our challenges tomorrow?

Try it for a month and see how it affects your daily emotional state.

3 **Your behaviour/actions.**

You can influence your thinking from the outside in. If you behave in a way consistent with a strengths-focused way of thinking, the behaviour will lead you to that mindset. So we will take you through the actions, behaviours and organisational processes that are consistent with a strengths-focused way of thinking. Read on, take the four steps in our MORE model, and you will find your thinking becoming increasingly strengths-focused.

4 **Your results.**

When you look at your results at work, be it day-to-day, week to week, month to month, or year to year, you can develop the habit of asking the questions we outlined above, that will build your strengths and your success.

With a focus on weakness, the process of reviewing results may be about 'Where are we not doing well enough? What's causing it? Who is responsible?'

With a focus on strengths the questions will be 'What did we achieve?' 'How did we achieve it?' 'What strengths did we use?' and 'How can we do even better next time?' We may also focus on 'What aspects did we enjoy most? Least? How can we make the experience more enjoyable next time?'

Where can I immediately apply this in my work?

When we are asked how to create a strengths-focused culture in an organisation or team, we often advise some simple small steps as the first step forward. These small steps involve small regular habits which help to embed a strengths-focused mindset.

Change creates change – small steps often lead to significant changes. Building on the ideas mentioned above, we offer you the following exercise, our five-day challenge. The three elements involve interactions on three levels – with yourself, in one-to-one conversations with your team members, and in meetings with your team. Take notes on your experience.

Exercise: Your five-day challenge

1. With myself

At the beginning of each day:

▌ Which of my strengths will make most difference to my results today?

At the end of each day:

▌ What were my best achievements today?

▌ What did I do well?

▌ Which achievements or successes did I enjoy most?

2. In one-to-one meetings with my team members

At the beginning of each meeting I will ask them:

▍ What have been your successes/achievements since we last met? (*Give feedback on strengths on show*)

At the end of each meeting:

▍ What was most useful (in our meeting)?

3. In team meetings

At the beginning of the meeting I will ask:

▍ What successes or achievements have you each had since our last meeting? (*Give feedback on strengths on show*)

At the end of the meeting:

▍ What have we achieved in this meeting?

▍ How can we make the next meeting even better?

These simple exercises encourage a strengths-focused mindset. Of course there may be the need to discuss weaknesses or problems. However, by beginning regular conversations with a focus on strength, we then 'find the energy to fix what is not working'. Make a note of your experiences.

My five-day challenge

What I did	The impact I noticed it had
With myself:	
In one-to-one meetings:	
In team meetings:	

The mindset of a strengths-focused leader

1 Do the five-day challenge and take the time to notice the impact of these strengths-focused habits.

2 Continue using the ones that are making a difference.

3 Notice the impact of these habits on your mindset as a leader.

4 Generally pay more attention to the way you talk about yourself and your team members. Raising your awareness of this will highlight your current mindset, affirm where it is already strong, and show you the opportunities to 'strengthen' it.

part

The MORE model

No man will find the best way to do a thing unless he loves to do that thing.
(Japanese proverb)

So you may by now be saying, 'Yes, I get the idea of strengths. I
understand that a focus on strengths and what's working is likely to create
a positive atmosphere in my team. I've tried the Five-day challenge you
set me in the last chapter. It seems to be making a difference but is that
it? What else do I do? I'm worried that if I don't have specific things that
I can do to implement all this, I'll gradually forget about it. The mindset
might fade away.'

These questions are typical of people who come to the idea of strengths,
like it, and then wonder how to make use of it. Part 2 answers these
important questions by presenting the **MORE** model.

The **MORE** model makes the connection between mindset and
behaviour, between idea and action. Employing the four steps of the
MORE model reinforces the strengths mindset. As this mindset is
reinforced, it starts to spontaneously drive your leadership behaviour.
Action reinforces mindset and then mindset further reinforces behaviour.

The **MORE** model gives you an easy to remember, four-step framework for comprehensively incorporating a strengths focus into everything that you do as a leader, to get the most out of your people, their potential and their performance.

You'll see from the following figure that all four steps of the **MORE** model are underpinned by the strengths-focused mindset we described in the last chapter.

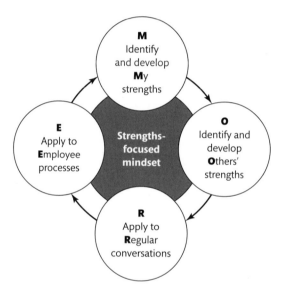

Supported by a strengths-focused mindset, establishing strengths in a team or organisation follows these four steps:

M Identify and develop <u>M</u>y strengths

The best way to fully understand a model you intend to use to manage and lead others is to first apply it to yourself. We'll show you the different options you have at your disposal to identify and fully exploit your own strengths, whilst managing any weaknesses or performance risks (in Chapter 3).

O Identify and develop Others' strengths

Once you have developed a good understanding of your own strengths and taken action to make more of them, you will be ready to explore how you can help others that you lead to do the same.

Different individuals in your team will have different strengths. They will increase their performance with a focus on building on their strengths, rather than focusing on their weaknesses. Your team will perform at its best if it fully exploits the strengths of each individual. We'll show you how you can introduce the approach to your team, and how you can then work with each individual to identify and develop their strengths (in Chapters 6, 7 and 8).

R **Apply a strengths focus to Regular conversations (one-to-ones, team meetings, coaching conversations)**

As we said above, a challenge to a newcomer to the strengths approach is about how to use it day-to-day. Your daily interactions and conversations with your team are often focused on setting and achieving performance goals, and monitoring progress towards them. Some of these interactions may happen in one-to-one conversations and some will happen in team or group discussions. We'll show you how to have strengths-focused interactions in all of your regular conversations at work (in Chapters 9, 10 and 11).

E **Apply a strengths focus to Employee processes (performance appraisal, development discussions and recruitment)**

As well as the day-to-day interactions that you have with your team, there are the formal employee processes that address the recruitment, performance appraisal and development of team members. These may vary from one organisation to another but, as research shows, they may be structured in ways that don't bring out the best performance. We will show you what strengths-focused performance appraisal looks like (Chapter 12), present a strengths approach to development discussions (Chapter 13), and show the significant benefit to the approach within recruitment (Chapter 14).

In the next three chapters we describe step 1 of the **MORE** model: identifying and developing **M**y strengths.

My strengths

What is necessary to change a person is to change his awareness of himself
(Abraham Maslow, psychologist)

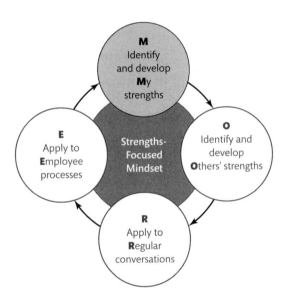

The '**M**' of the **MORE** model stands for 'Identify and develop <u>My</u> strengths'.

If you have done any self-awareness work as a leader, we're sure you will agree that the more you understand yourself – your qualities, strengths, motivations, preferences, attitudes and weaknesses – and how you are different from and similar to others, the more able you are to understand, interact and influence others effectively.

The 'M' of the **MORE** model invites you into that self-awareness exercise. The next three chapters will help you to be more aware of your own strengths and weaknesses, and how to play to your strengths more, and manage your weaknesses from strength.

We have shown a range of evidence on the benefits of doing this (in Chapter 1). It will raise your own performance and satisfaction with your work.

And as a leader, this increased self-awareness will also enable you to support those you lead to make that same journey, raising their performance and engagement.

It will enable you to get the best from those you lead.

So, in this part of the book we will cover:

1   Identifying **M**y own strengths (and weaknesses) (Chapter 3)

2   Developing **M**y strengths and managing **M**y weaknesses (Chapter 4)

3   Aligning **M**y goals and objectives with **M**y strengths (Chapter 5)

Identifying **M**y own strengths

*Everyone has been made for some particular work, and the
desire for that work has been put in every heart.*
(Rumi, 13th-century Persian poet, jurist, theologian, and Sufi mystic)

IN THE PREVIOUS TWO CHAPTERS we explained what a strengths focus is
and why it's important, and we also presented the mindset of a strengths-
focused leader. In this chapter we'll invite you to think about what your
strengths are, those things you do really well and feel energised by when
you do them. You may have already begun to do this.

Similarly, you may have already pinpointed some of your weaknesses,
those things that drain you when you do them and that you don't excel at.

By the end of this chapter you will be clear about the following:

1. What are the range of strengths that people have?
2. What are the five different methods I can use to identify my strengths
   (and weaknesses)?
3. Method 1: Strength spotting
4. Method 2: Weakness spotting
5. Method 3: The 5 Step Strengths Map
6. Method 4: 360 degree feedback
7. Method 5: Online strengths assessments

What are the range of strengths that people have?

Before we invite you to identify your strengths we'd like to share our experience of the range of strengths that people have, and some of the words they might use to describe them.

You'll see later in this chapter that the online tools for identifying strengths use a pre-determined list or menu of strengths. The strengths that they help you identify will be ones from their list. Each of the four online tools uses a different vocabulary.

If you have done some work already on identifying your strengths you may have your own favourite words to describe them, and that's absolutely fine.

Our experience is that those coming to strengths identification for the first time appreciate some help in thinking about what the range of personality strengths might be and the range of words that could be used to describe them.

So we present you with our own dictionary of strengths on page 37 below. This comes from viewing the range of ways strengths are described by the different tools and writers. They also take account of our context of workplace strengths and leadership.

We have grouped the strengths into four categories: our strengths in the way we think, in the way we handle our emotions, in the way we communicate with and influence others, and in the way we take action and get things done (execution).

You'll see that all four of these categories contain strengths that deliver results in the workplace. No one needs to have all of these strengths. In fact no great leader does. However, it's very useful for you to know which ones you do have, and how you might ensure that the others are covered, even if it's not by you.

We'll invite you to do various exercises in the rest of this chapter. You may want to refer back to our dictionary of strengths to help you clarify your thinking. You can download and print it onto one page at our website www.sfleadership.co.uk, and it's also shown in our Appendix. You can use the actual words we use, or you can use our list merely to stimulate your thinking, whilst using your own words to describe your strengths.

A dictionary of strengths

THINKING STRENGTHS

Analytical Thinking	Using logic, objectivity and critical thinking.
Common Sense	Taking a practical, down-to-earth approach to thinking through challenges.
Creativity	Coming up with new and innovative ideas.
Curiosity	Interested to seek out new ideas, ways of thinking and facts.
Detail Focus	Focusing on the specific facts and details in a situation.
Reflection	Thinking things through in depth on one's own.
Strategic Thinking	Focusing on the longer term, bigger picture view; seeing patterns and themes across current and future challenges.

EMOTIONAL STRENGTHS

Courage	Taking on difficult and challenging situations.
Drive	The motivation to push forward with challenges and goals.
Emotional Awareness	Being aware in the now of one's own and other's emotions.
Emotional Balance	Remaining calm in varied circumstances.
Enthusiasm	Having energy and passion.
Optimism	Seeing the best possibilities in any situation.
Persistence	Sticking at it regardless of the challenges.
Resilience	Handling continuous pressure in one's stride and bouncing back positively.
Self-confidence	A strong belief in oneself and one's ability.

COMMUNICATING AND INFLUENCING STRENGTHS

Collaboration	Working well with others in joint endeavours.
Communicator	Communicating ideas effectively to others face to face.

Developer	Developing others well.
Empathy	Recognising and appreciating the emotions of others.
Fairness	Treating every individual fairly.
Harmony	Creating harmony and positive feelings in others.
Humour	Generating humour and fun in a way that enables effective interactions.
Inclusion	Including others appropriately in a situation.
Leader	Stepping into a leadership role in situations.
Listener	Hearing the ideas, views and emotions of others in a way that ensures they feel listened to.
Motivator	Energising others towards a goal.
Persuasiveness	Convincing others towards a particular idea or way of seeing things.
Relationship Builder	Building new relationships.
Writer	Writing in a way that effectively communicates a message.

ACTION AND EXECUTION STRENGTHS

Adaptability	Changing plans quickly when needed to achieve results.
Decisiveness	Taking decisions in a timely manner, when needed.
Efficiency	Getting things done in the time frame.
Initiative	Stepping up and getting on with what is needed.
Organiser	Organising practicalities in complex situations.
Planner	Creating workable plans to achieve the desired results.
Problem Solver	Solving problems that stand in the way of the desired results.
Results Focus	Maintaining focus on the result required and staying headed in that direction.
Self-Improvement	Improving one's knowledge, skills and ways of thinking to improve results.

What are the five different methods I can use to identify my strengths (and weaknesses)?

For someone new to the exercise of identifying your strengths, exploring your options can be a confusing activity. A Google search on the phrase 'strength assessment' will give you more than 70 million results!

However, the good news is that there are five straightforward methods to identify your own strengths and weaknesses. They are:

1. **Strength spotting.** This method is about paying attention to your energy levels as you do various activities, and so begin to build up clarity about the things you do that **energise** you. It is also about paying attention to what you say about the various aspects of your work.

2. **Weakness spotting.** Similarly this method is about paying attention to your energy levels as you do various activities, and so begin to build up clarity about the things you do that **drain** you.

3. **The 5 Step Strengths Map.** Either working on your own or with someone else to ask you the relevant questions, this method involves doing a semi-structured written self-assessment.

4. **360 degree feedback.** This method involves using feedback from others to determine the things you are good at that energise you.

5. **Online strengths assessment**. Using an online questionnaire to identify strengths and weaknesses. We describe four in particular:

   - Realise2©: www.realise2.com

   - Strengthscope™: www.strengthscope.com

   - StrengthsFinder™: www.strengthsfinder.com

   - Values In Action: www.viacharacter.org

You'll notice that as you go from number 1 to number 5 above that the process becomes more structured. We will look at each of these in more detail.

We start with the simplest approach to identifying your own strengths. This is something you can do easily, with a fairly simple set of instructions. You could then go on to use the more complex approaches. These will then refine your thinking on the exact nature of your strengths.

Method 1: Strength spotting

Strength spotting is the most straightforward, informal and unstructured of our methods. Put very simply it involves paying attention to our energy levels when we are involved in different activities.

We'll look at three areas to apply this to:

1. your work right now;
2. your work in the past;
3. your experiences outside of work.

We'll start by inviting you to do an exercise throughout your next day at work.

Your work right now

Here is a challenge for you after you wake up tomorrow morning (or the next work day). Pay attention to yourself as you go through the day. After you get up and your thoughts drift towards the working day ahead of you, notice which activities you are looking forward to doing. Then when you get to work pay attention to your energy levels and enthusiasm levels as you go through the day.

As you go from activity to activity, which are the ones that:

- you really love doing?
- you get a real buzz from?
- time flies when you are doing them?
- you feel 'in the flow' while doing?
- are the things about which you would say 'this is the real me'?
- you enjoy learning about and learn very easily?
- you would fill your 'ideal' day at work doing?
- make you feel some of the following emotions: passionate, strong, enthusiastic, motivated, confident, natural, on fire, high, great, authentic, in the zone, powerful?
- you talk about with more energy in your voice, and look more animated to others when you talk about them and do them?

Exercise

Make a list of these activities. As you do this, you may become more consciously aware of how much your current job is satisfying you and which parts of your job give you most satisfaction. But just thinking about the things that energise you is not the full story. There are some other aspects that need to be considered.

As you look at the list of activities, or as you think about those things that energise you, there is one more element to consider. Which of these activities do you perform really well?

You will have your own views of this. Would others agree with you? Only you can really know which things energise you. However, you will need corroboration from others on which activities you perform really well. So for each of the activities that energise you, check how strongly you can agree with the following statements:

1   I have experienced great results at this type of activity.

2   My performance records at work show great results in this activity.

3   Other people tell me (360 degree feedback, etc.) that I have a real aptitude for this type of activity.

4   I have received recognition or awards for doing this type of activity.

You'll want to have strongly agreed with at least a couple of the statements above for you to be able to call this a strength.

Exercise

Write down the activities that fit both of the criteria for you – you love doing it and you perform it really well. Feel free to use our dictionary of strengths to help you.

If you are doing a job that really suits you, you will probably have found this exercise both easy to do and enjoyable.

But what if you are doing a job that you currently don't enjoy very much? It may have been very difficult for you to notice any experiences of being energised at work. If so, there are the other two areas to explore to spot your strengths. These two areas will also give you further confirmation of your strengths.

Your work in the past

Think back to other jobs or roles that you have had, that you particularly enjoyed. Think of specific work situations where you were doing something you are good at, that you really enjoyed, and that you were getting good results from. Let's take an example to clarify this.

In the real world . . .

When I (Mike) coached Bill he was Head of IT in a large public sector organisation. He hadn't enjoyed the job for some years. His own boss, the Director of Corporate Services, was beginning to ask Bill some awkward questions about his performance in the role. When I suggested that Bill pay attention to his energy level over the next week and let me know about the times he was most energised, he came to our next session with a sense of frustration. 'That was really hard,' he said. 'It really dawned on me. There is almost nothing about this role that I really enjoy.'

So I then asked Bill about his past experiences of work – the different jobs and roles he'd had over the years.

'Bill, can you tell me about the situations at work that you remember where you were really enjoying the work you were doing, and you were really good at it, and you got great results?' I asked him. Bill was clear: 'Yeah that's easy,' he said. 'It was the first few years working here, before I got promoted to team leader. Leading people doesn't suit me, and it took me away from what I loved. In those days I was taking on practical projects every few months, upgrading a department's machines, things like that. I loved it. I could get on with it myself, and I got a real sense of satisfaction from getting clear practical results. I also had a phase taking on problems reported to the help desk, and I really enjoyed the troubleshooting. Not knowing what was coming next and being flexible about responding to the different priorities – it was just fun for me.'

These conversations helped Bill re-evaluate his future working life. His current job didn't suit him.

Exercise

Write down situations at work in the past, where you were really motivated, engaged and energised, and where you were performing really well and getting good results. What were you doing?

Your experiences outside of work

The things that energise you outside of work often point towards your inherent strengths. Here is a real example, once again with Bill.

As part of our further exploration of Bill's strengths I invited him to notice what he currently (and in the past) felt energised to do outside of work that he felt he was good at. Next time I saw him, he had a grin on his face as I asked him how he had got on. 'Well, that was much easier,' he said. 'I was really in my element at the weekend, taking time to think through and plan a big DIY project I have taken on, building cupboards in our spare bedroom. Once I had my project plan, it got even better – I got my hands dirty getting on with it. I was in there almost the whole day on my own and I loved it. I knew what I had to do, I had thought every step through, and I had clear practical tasks to get done to achieve it. While I was doing it, I noticed a leak in a central heating pipe. That was even better. I got to do a bit of troubleshooting.'

Bill's current role wasn't suiting him – he had no opportunities to do the detailed project planning and the practical troubleshooting that he had natural aptitude for and that he loved doing. His current role was a much more strategic one, interacting with the other Heads, networking with other stakeholders – very much an extrovert, influencing role.

His current role didn't fill him with joy. It wasn't accessing his untapped strengths (Problem Solver, Detail Focus, Efficiency, Organiser, Planner, Adaptability), which he hadn't used for some years now. And he wasn't performing very well at it. It called for a different set of strengths. Bill started to build a plan to set up his own business, offering IT services to small businesses. The last time I heard from him he was thriving. He was doing what he does best – playing to his strengths.

Exercise

Write down the things that you do outside of work that you are really good at and that energise you.

Seeing what you've written will give you more clarity on where your inherent strengths lie. Comparing these to what you do in your current job may offer extra insights about how well your current work suits you. Do those things outside of work energise you more, and are you better at them, as in Bill's case? That may well give you useful ideas about where your future career will ideally lie. Of course you may also notice the same strengths appearing in both places, which suggests that your current work will be playing well to your strengths.

If you have engaged in the exercises above, you may see how this will be helpful to you as a leader. Not only will you be clear about where you are likely to find your best performance, but you may also have begun to notice that you can do this same 'noticing' exercise with the people around you in your team. We'll come back to that later (in Chapter 7), when you will look at identifying and developing strengths in others.

How important is the context in which I use my strengths?

For some people a strength maybe be sharply defined by the context within which they use it. For others the context may be less important. Here are two examples to clarify this point.

In the real world . . .

Anya did the exercises we mention above. She identified a Communicator 's strengths when in front of groups. She loved doing it and got great feedback about how well she did it. As we discussed it, I (Mike) asked her, 'Does it matter who you are communicating to, or what you are communicating about, or when or where or how you are doing it? Would you get the same energy from presenting about anything, and to any kind of audience?' She thought this through and we unpicked her strength a bit further. Anya worked for a charity in the field of Cancer Care. She particularly liked speaking and presenting to groups of patients. She had presented to other audiences and was fairly good at this but it didn't energise her in the same way. So her strength is in presenting to groups of patients, rather than just simply presenting. To her this is very important.

I also coached Sanjit. He had years of experience in three completely different sectors, and part of his role was to facilitate team-building events to other organisations. It didn't matter to Sanjit who the team was. In fact he liked the variety of working with different teams from different sectors. He also didn't at all mind what the topics were that the team focused on. Once again he quite liked the variety he experienced with different teams. He had done team-building work in lots of different situations, times and places, and in lots of different styles from formal to informal. None of this mattered to him.

Exercise

Think about each of the strengths you have identified so far and ask the five questions about each: who, what, where, when and how?

1. Does it matter **who** I do this activity with or for?

2. Does it matter **what** this activity is about?

3. Does it matter **where** I do this activity?

4 Does it matter **when** I do this activity?

5 Does it matter **how** I am required to do it? Are there different ways?

Make your notes.

The strength	What matters in the context?

Being clear on these questions was particularly helpful to Anya. When I coached her on her future career moves, this contextual detail about her Communicator strength when presenting helped her to clarify her best options.

For one of us, the context for creativity is very important. I (Kathy) love to be engaged in creative thinking and design work, but only find it really energising when I am doing it with others. It doesn't energise me in the same way if I do it on my own. No surprise then that I am co-authoring this book with Mike!

Method 2: Weakness spotting

If you took our challenge to notice what energises you at work, here is the opposite challenge for you. Pay attention to yourself as you go through the day. After you get up and your thoughts drift towards the working day ahead of you, notice which activities you are *not* looking forward to doing. When you get to work pay attention to your energy and enthusiasm levels as you go through the day.

As you go from activity to activity, which are the ones that:

▌ always drain your energy?

▌ you look for any excuse to avoid?

▌ time drags for you when you are doing them?

▌ you feel exhausted after doing them for any significant length of time?

▌ are the things about which you would say 'this really isn't me'?

▌ your 'ideal' day at work would definitely not include?

▌ make you feel some of the following emotions: bored, restless, distracted, de-energised, weak, frustrated, irritated, out of sorts.

▌ you talk about with low energy in your voice, and look de-energised to others when you talk about them, or are involved in doing them.

Exercise

Make a list of those activities.

As you look at your list, or as you think about those things that de-energise you at work, there is the other side of the strengths equation to consider. Which of these activities do you perform well, and which do you perform badly at?

Take your list from the last exercise above and make notes under the two headings below.

These activities drain me even though I am good at them.	These activities drain me, and I am not good at them.

So here we have two categories of activities:

1 **Your learned behaviours.** These are the things that over the years you've managed to get good at, even although you get drained doing them for any significant amount of time. In developing your strengths, you obviously want to look at how you can do less of these activities and more of those that energise you. More of this later (in Chapter 4).

2 **Your weaknesses.** These are the things that not only drain you, but that you don't perform well at. These activities make you feel weak. It is important to recognise these for two reasons. First, if it is a weakness that significantly impacts on your performance, you will want to address this as a priority. We'll look at how you can tackle weaknesses in a strengths-focused way (in Chapter 4). Secondly, if the weakness is not critical to your success in your role, you'll want to be clear on how much energy to put into managing it. (Again, Chapter 4 will clarify this.)

So by now you should be clear about the kind of activities that see you playing to your strengths, and how much of those you are tapping into in your current job role. You should also be clear about the activities that drain you, whether or not you can perform them well.

Activities involving strengths and weaknesses

One further thing to consider is activities or projects that may involve a combination of both strengths and weaknesses.

Let's take a couple of examples.

In the real world . . .

Ben was Financial Director of a UK firm, which had been expanding for a few years. As the firm grew larger and more complex, Ben felt the need to give more guidance to department heads and team leaders around budget setting. He decided to create a Microsoft Excel spreadsheet that would take the headache out of the process for the relevant managers, whilst also ensuring that they came up with budgets that Ben wouldn't have to spend hours getting his team to tidy up.

Although it was a job he could easily outsource, Ben had enjoyed hours of fun on Excel over the years (yes, some people do!), and wanted to do it himself. It wouldn't take him long – he enjoyed it so much he even found himself doing it at the weekend. He was very adept at stretching the program into new and intricate functions, formulae and specialised accounting tasks.

The project had two phases. The first one was about design – deciding on the overall structure of the spreadsheet. How many separate sheets did it need? How would they connect together? How would the user step their way through them?

The second phase was about implementing that design – painstakingly programming each cell with the right formula, and programming each of the buttons that enabled the user to step through the process one step at a time.

Ben got restless during phase 1. The broader thinking needed during this design phase wasn't enjoyable for him, even though he did it fairly well. He couldn't wait to get on to phase 2, where he got a real pleasure from the practical programming work with each small element of the spreadsheet file.

Ben's strength was in the accuracy of fine Detail Focus and Efficiency in the programming. It wasn't in the bigger picture, up-front design work (Creativity and Strategic Thinking).

Here is another example. This time it's my own (Mike).

> **In the real world . . .**
>
> Fifteen years ago I took on a challenging project. Using Microsoft Access I set about designing a database that would track the activity and outcomes of the team that I led.
>
> As I got started I was in my element. 'What are all the great things we could get it to do?' I thought. 'What if we could just click a button and get performance reports?' What about using it to track stakeholder feedback, staff development records, and . . .' I was really buzzing. For a few days I was so excited by the possibilities that I didn't sleep that well. I kept waking up with some new exciting idea that kept my mind ticking over. Eventually I decided on the overall structure of the database: the types of tables, forms, queries and reports it would have and the interrelationships of the parts. A great sense of satisfaction came over me as I realised that the design had in it everything we needed it to do. That's where most of the fun stopped for me. Now I had the chore of (Detail Focus and Efficiency) programming each small element to create the final product.
>
> My strength was in the bigger picture (Creativity and Strategic Thinking). It wasn't in the fine detail of the individual small elements. In fact I had to really push myself to get that side of it done well. I did a lot of error-checking to ensure I hadn't missed anything. I found lots of small errors, but through dogged persistence ensured that the final product worked as expected.

As you can see, Ben and I could have gone into business as a double act! I would do the design and he would do the implementation. We will give you more on that idea of complementary role-sharing later (in Chapter 4). For now, the examples illustrate the idea that certain activities or projects call for a mixture of strengths. Sometimes we may have only some of the strengths, and sometimes we may have all the strengths required.

Our earlier example of Anya, working in the Cancer Care charity, was also an example of someone using a combination of two strengths in an activity that demanded them both. Anya had worked with patients for many years, and had great empathy for them. Empathy was a strength for her as well as the Communicating and Presenting that we mentioned earlier. This particular work of presenting to groups of patients allowed her to use both strengths, which was even more fulfilling for Anya.

So you now know the basics of strength spotting. Next we'll look at how you can identify and define your strengths in a slightly more structured and more comprehensive way. This may be important for you at work when a formal development plan is needed, both for yourself or for those you lead.

Method 3: The 5 Step Strengths Map

Guided by our experience of using a variety of tools, we have developed a simple semi-structured process for comprehensively identifying your strengths and weaknesses using the following five steps:

Steps 1–3: The activities that energise you

1. **Your strengths.** The things that you are good at, that energise and motivate you *and* get you great results. You'll want to make the most of these.

2. **Your untapped strengths.** The strengths that you don't use as much as you would want to. These are an area of huge potential for you.

3. **Your strengths overplayed.** If there are times when you use a strength too much or in an inappropriate context, such that it is having a negative impact, we call this a 'strength overplayed'. You'll want to focus on using the right strength, in the right amount, in the right situation.

Steps 4–5: The activities that drain your energy

4. **Your learned behaviours.** The things you do well that don't energise you, and that drain you. You'll want to reduce the amount of time that these occupy you.

5. **Your weaknesses.** The things you don't perform well and that drain you when you do them. You'll want to be clear about how best to respond to these, particularly if they are critical to your work-based goals.

In the rest of this chapter we'll help you take these five steps. We'll first of all show you an example of someone using the process then we'll invite you to do it. It involves you answering some simple but powerful questions to explore your own experience and clarify your understanding.

Once you've done the exercise to identify your strengths we'll be in a position to help you decide how to make the most of them. (We'll do this in Chapter 4.)

Our next example looks at how someone does the self-assessment process. Meet Mary.

In the real world . . .

Mary is the leader of a Scientific Projects team in a pharmaceutical company. She was previously in a very technical role for seven years, being involved in medical research and product trials with a variety of customers and stakeholders in her sector. She has relished the opportunity to step into a leadership role, and has led her team now for two years. She has settled into the role well and has been offered coaching for her ongoing development. I (Mike) explained the 5 Step Strengths Map process to her and invited her to bring the completed set of questions to our next session. She used our Dictionary of Strengths to help her define her strengths. Here are the questions and her answers.

5 Step Strengths Map – Steps 1–3: The activities that energise you

Step 1: Your strengths

▌ What do you love doing in your work?
(Think about your current job and jobs you've had in the past. Identify times and specific situations when you were really energised by what you were doing.)

> *Mary's answer:* I love doing the longer term and big picture thinking about our team – having a blank piece of paper and seeing what appears on it when I ask myself 'Where is the industry going?' and 'What could we get involved in that would add most value?' It's been a breath of fresh air for me to move into the leadership role. I suddenly realise, as I'm thinking this through, that my more technical role that I had for seven years didn't allow me to do much of these things that I really love doing. So I suppose the strengths here are Strategic Thinking and Creativity. People tell me I have a robust and sharp-minded way of thinking things through so I suppose being Analytical Thinking is a strength too.

▌**What behaviours and attributes do you enjoy using and demonstrate well and use regularly?**

Mary's answer: When I think of the feedback I've had over the last couple of years I guess the three I've mentioned above have been highlighted. Apart from those, I think I'm pretty good at focusing on getting things done. I do get a real buzz out of that. So I guess you could call that Results Focus.

Also I really like building relationships. I guess that's what may have drawn me to the role in the first place, the opportunity to build relationships with the customers. Now it's different – it's about building great relationships with the team and beyond and a bit less with the customers, but the strength is the same I think: Relationship Builder.

I've also had feedback that I am good at influencing people, that's Persuasiveness and I have to say, I do really enjoy doing that. I was trained in it, but even before that I think I had a good intuitive idea about how to do it.

I'm told that I have a strength in attention to detail, your Detail Focus, but I have to say it's not something that energises me like it does other people. Feels more like a chore. So I guess I shouldn't include that one as it doesn't fit your definition of a strength. I'd really rather someone else did the checking of the detail, dotting the I's and crossing the T's.

▌**When do you use these strengths? What examples can you think of?**

Mary's answer: I guess I've answered that above with some of them. I think I use Results Focus everywhere I go. In meetings, in one-to-ones with my team, in the strategic planning exercises I get invited to, and in my own development. Like now!! With Influencing, it's probably anywhere where I sense that we are not heading in the same direction, a team member, or a peer. Even with my own manager, I manage to do a bit of managing upwards (but don't tell him!).

With Analytical Thinking I find that I want to unpick both sides of an idea when we are looking at what next steps to take from a number of options in a project.

The Relationship Builder is with anyone I have identified as a key stakeholder (is that my Results Focus again?) With Creativity and Strategic Thinking, I book a meeting with myself for an hour every Monday afternoon. I get out the office to a café down the road, and I take my notebook. I look at the bigger projects that are further down the line, and I draw mind maps about everything that occurs to me. I can't tell you how much I enjoy doing it. And it's so useful in getting good results for our team in the long run. I also use it in the quarterly team meetings we have that look at our progress on the annual goals.

▌**What do you enjoy about using them? How do they make you feel?**

Mary's answer: I've probably answered a lot of this in the previous questions. When I'm doing Strategic Thinking and being Creative it feels like fun rather than work. With Persuasiveness it feels like an energising challenge and there's a real pleasure of achievement when I use Results Focus and know that this focus will mean that we'll succeed. I think I also get a buzz from Analytical Thinking, that enjoyment of looking at all the possibilities and getting a well thought through idea out of the other end – I like a good debate. With Relationship Builder I think I get just a natural pleasure from building relationships with other people and getting on well with them. I suppose underneath I know I'll get better results if we get on better, and I'll be able to influence them easier. But apart from all that, I still just enjoy building relationships for the enjoyment of it.

Step 2: Your untapped strengths

▌**What do you love doing but just don't get the opportunity to do very often? Perhaps strengths you used in previous jobs or roles?**

Mary's answer: Actually it was really interesting to think about this one. In my previous role my manager was really keen on development and was always giving me new projects that stretched me and offering me training and development opportunities. I really loved that. I guess it is about learning or growth, which I see as Self-Improvement. I even got opportunities to pass it on to the others in the team, which I also enjoyed. Is that the same strength or is that Developer? There has been a bit of that in the new role, but really nothing like it used to be. I think I'd get a lot from doing more of those.

▌ **When do you currently use this strength/these strengths?**

Mary's answer: The first few months of the new role had a steep
learning curve and I enjoyed that challenge, but it's eased off since
then. I realise that as I'm thinking about this, and although I have
made time for reviewing goals with the team, I haven't really set
aside much development time with them.

▌ **What do you enjoy about using it? How does it make you feel?**

Mary's answer: Being involved in learning really does feel like
growing to me. It's about making more of myself, then I can offer
others more as well. It feels really fulfilling.

▌ **On a scale of 0–10, where 0 is not at all and 10 is ideal, how much do
you currently use that strength?**

Mary's answer: Mmm. Probably only at a 3 at the moment.

Step 3: Your overplayed strengths

▌ **Where might you be using some of your strengths too much?**

Mary's answer: I realised when I was answering the question about
my untapped strengths that I may be overusing my Results Focus
strength. I think I need to balance it a bit more, maybe with more of
the Self-Improvement strength.

▌ **What's the impact?**

Mary's answer: I think it may de-motivate some in my team, with all
of my focus on the numbers and the targets. It may lead them to feel
under-valued and under-developed.

▌ **Where might it be the wrong kind of situation to use any of your
strengths?**

Mary's answer: I think with my strength of Strategic Thinking, I have
to be careful I don't go off into using that strength when the team and
I need to be focusing on the day-to-day results. I need to save it for
my café meetings with myself, and for the quarterly reviews of our
annual targets. Day-to-day it's more about the short-term priorities.
I notice that when I have overplayed the Strategic Thinking that
the team get frustrated with me. They have a more short-term focus
generally, which they need to have most of the time.

5 Step Strengths Map – Steps 4–5: The activities that drain your energy

Step 4: Your learned behaviours

▌ What are you good at, but don't enjoy, or that drains your energy?

Mary's answer: Yeah, I probably answered this one above. People have commented that I have good attention to detail. But I don't enjoy that. If the result is important I force myself to do it. But I don't really enjoy it. I'd rather be in the café having some really useful creative ideas, and a latte!

▌ What sort of things do you struggle to get started with?

Mary's answer: It is when it's a task that is about a lot of focus on detail. Those things can sit on my to-do list for a long time.

Step 5: Your weaknesses

▌ What do you perform less well in and also find to be a drain on your energy?

Mary's answer: I think I have a weakness around Communicator. I sometimes don't get the point over clearly enough. I know what I mean, but the people listening to me don't. I like a fast pace, and maybe don't slow down enough for people to stay with me. It's been mentioned in 360 degree feedback a few times. And I maybe also have a weakness around Empathy. I like building relationships, but I'm not so good when someone is moaning. I tend to get impatient with them. Interestingly it hasn't been mentioned in 360 degree feedback in the past. Maybe I hide it well!

▌ How does this weakness currently impact your role and work?

Mary's answer: With Communicator it shows itself at team meetings when I've presented something to the team and they look a bit confused, like I haven't made the point clearly enough. With Empathy, I'm not sure how much of an impact it has, though I'll probably work on it anyway. Maybe there are a couple of people in the team I could show more empathy to.

▌ How important is it to your success in the role?

Mary's answer: I think Communicator is really important. There are some important messages I need to get across clearly – our performance targets could depend on it, so what I need to do is prepare more and be more patient. With Empathy it probably doesn't matter all that much. So I'll be interested to see what you say about the best way to approach these.

So Mary's 5 Step Strengths Map looks like this:

Steps 1–3: The activities that energise you

1. Your strengths	**2. Your untapped strengths**	**3. Your overplayed strengths**
▮ Strategic Thinking ▮ Creativity ▮ Analytical Thinking ▮ Results Focus ▮ Relationship Builder ▮ Persuasiveness	▮ Self-improvement ▮ Developer	▮ Results Focus ▮ Strategic Thinking

Steps 4–5: The activities that drain your energy

4. Your learned behaviours	**5. Your weaknesses**
▮ Detail Focus	▮ Communicator ▮ Empathy

Mary then went on to look at how she could make the most of her strengths, and how best to manage her weaknesses. This process is covered in the next chapter.

Now it's your turn. Use our dictionary of strengths if you wish, and jot down your answers to the questions.

Exercise: Your 5 Step Strengths Map

Use the map to capture your responses to the questions and 'map' your strengths. See if you can identify up to six or seven main strengths, and a similar number of untapped strengths. It is usual to identify no more than three or four weaknesses. If you find more, you're trying too hard!

Your 5 Step Strengths Map

Steps 1–3: The activities that energise you

1. Your strengths

- What do you love doing in your work? (*Think back to situations you have been most energised at work*)
- What behaviours and attributes do you enjoy using, demonstrate well and use regularly?
- When do you use these strengths? What examples can you think of?
- What do you enjoy about using them? How do they make you feel?

2. Your untapped strengths

- What do you love doing but just don't get the opportunity to do very often? Perhaps strengths you used in previous jobs or roles?
- When do you currently use this strength/these strengths?
- What do you enjoy about using it? How does it make you feel?
- On a scale of 0–10, where 0 is not all and 10 is ideal, how much do you currently use that strength?

3. Your overplayed strengths

- Where might you be using some of your strengths too much?
- What's the impact?
- Where might it be the wrong kind of situation to use them?

Steps 4–5: The activities that drain your energy

4. Your learned behaviours

- What things are you good at, but don't enjoy or that drain you to do them?
- What sort of things do you struggle to get started with?

5. Your weaknesses

- What do you perform less well in and also find to be a drain on your energy?
- How does this weakness currently impact your role and work?
- How important is it to your success in the role?

Having completed your 5 Step Strengths Map you may want to go straight to the next chapter to look at how to make the most of your strengths and manage any significant weaknesses.

Or if you are interested in the other two ways to identify your strengths, read on.

Method 4: 360 degree feedback system

Research has shown that individuals aren't always the best judge of what they are good at, or where their weaknesses are.[1] Whereas I can be the best judge of what energises me, I may not be the best judge of what I am good at, because this requires corroboration by others.

The value of feedback

So we often encourage the leaders we work with to think about getting feedback from those around them in order to validate their own ideas. You'll see later in this chapter that this could be done via one of the online strengths assessments. Another way to establish what others see you as good at might be via your organisation's 360 degree feedback system. For those not familiar with this, it is where others are invited to rate your performance against a set of competencies judged to be the ones that are required in your role. The people usually asked to rate you are your line manager, some or all of your team members, some of your peers, and some of your other stakeholders. You should be able to see fairly easily the areas that people feel you are best at, and whether there are any significant weaknesses for you to be aware of.

How to ask for feedback

If your company does not have a 360 degree feedback system or competency framework, you could still get very useful input from others, possibly the same set of people we mentioned above, by asking them a few straightforward questions, such as:

1. What strengths do you feel I possess?

2. Which of them am I making best use of in your opinion?

3. Are there any key strengths I could make more of, in order to make a more powerful contribution?

4. Are there any significant weaknesses from your point of view, that are creating a significant performance risk? What can I do about them?

---

[1] Zenger, J. H., et al. (2012) *How to Be Exceptional: Drive leadership success by magnifying your strengths*, New York, McGraw-Hill.

5 Do you have any suggestions for how to make the most of my strengths?

6 Are any strengths being overplayed? Do you have any suggestions on what I could do?

Of course an exercise like this may need some careful preparation. You might like to think about the following:

▌ Who are the best people to ask?

▌ How will you prepare them and invite them to be honest?

▌ How will they feel about giving you feedback, especially if you are their manager?

▌ Are you ready to receive honest feedback?

▌ Are they ready to give it to you?

▌ Sharing with them that you intend to create a development plan as a result of your reflections on their feedback.

This feedback will then give you some very useful 'external' confirmation of the things you think you are good at, that seem to be getting you the best results, as well as any significant weaknesses. It is then a question of you deciding which of the things that you are good at are also strengths, by identifying those you love doing most and are most energised by. You may also then decide if you have any significant weaknesses.

Getting this feedback might actually be a useful activity to engage in before completing the 5 Step Strengths Map, since it may give you greater clarity about what you are good at.

Having done the exercise of identifying your strengths, on your own or with the help of others, you may want to go straight on to look at how to make the most of your strengths, and how to manage any significant weaknesses (in Chapter 4). This may also be very useful to you in considering how your strengths relate to those that research has suggested are key to effective leadership.

Alternatively, if you are interested in hearing about the last and most structured way to identify your strengths, by using an online strengths assessment, then carry on reading this chapter.

Method 5: Online strengths assessment

The four structured online assessments that we look at in this chapter are the work of strengths experts, usually psychologists, who have studied human personality and, from their studies, drawn up a list of human strengths. When you use one of their assessments you get the benefit of their work in separating out your different strengths into a framework that covers a spectrum of strengths across the full span of personality.

The assessment process

Through asking a series of questions, the assessment process helps you to identify your strengths from a pre-established menu, or list of strengths. For each strength in the menu you are essentially asked 'How good at this are you?' and 'How much do you enjoy doing this?' In some of the processes there is also an additional question, 'How often are you doing this?'

So without too much work from you in understanding and unpicking the human personality, you get to identify your key strengths and, with some of the models, your weaknesses also.

How valid and reliable are they?

You may ask, 'How accurate and dependable are these tools?' Well, all four models profess to have 'validity' and 'reliability' credentials. Validity is about whether an assessment actually does measure what it says it measures. Reliability is about whether you'll get consistent results from different questions that intend to measure the same strength, and consistent results if you retake the test within a short period of time.

The benefits

The benefits of this kind of assessment are:

1. You take advantage of someone else's work in presenting a broad framework of human strengths without too much work on your part.

2. You are likely to feel that you have a thorough and comprehensive view of your strengths, more so than if you only base your self-assessment on your own personal reflections on the question 'What are my strengths?'

3 To some extent it gives you an external input into understanding who you are. You are viewing yourself through someone else's lens of personality strengths. This can be very useful to you in gaining new insights about yourself.

4 At the time of writing, one of the assessment models, Strengthscope™, includes the opportunity to have 360 degree feedback from others. In this 360 degree view, you hear how others are seeing you use your strengths.

5 Three assessment models (Strengthscope™, Realise2© and VIA [*Pro version*]), also have the ability to produce a summary report for a whole team. As a leader of a team this can be invaluable to you, and to your team, in understanding how to get the best from the collection of individual strengths.

Finally, we feel it is important to say that an online tool is not an absolute necessity for you to identify and understand your strengths. Our own 5 Step Strengths Map will do a thorough and competent job, particularly where you have the opportunity to talk the questions through with someone else – be that a coach, colleague, or line manager, or someone else who knows you well.

However, with your interest sparked, you may value the opportunity to see what extra insights and self-awareness an online tool may offer you.

In the real world . . .

Vivien was going to an interview the following week. It was acting-up into her boss's role, while he was on a secondment.

For Vivien this was a huge opportunity to get herself new knowledge, experience and skills at a higher level, which would stand her in good stead when she would go for a permanent role at that level in the next year or so. This was important to her. She knew that the interviewers would quiz her about what she thought she could bring to the role, and where her challenges would be.

She called me (Mike), asking for a coaching session to prepare her for this line of questioning. I suggested an online strengths assessment ahead of our coaching session. The coaching session then focused on helping Vivien understand where she was currently using her key strengths and how she could play to these more fully in the new role. We also explored whether any significant weaknesses could show up in the new role, and how she could manage these.

> 'I can't tell you how valuable that was,' she said. 'I felt so much more confident going into the interview. I felt like I had a much broader understanding of myself and what I am capable of. Not only that, I now feel so much more confident about how I am now going to approach the role.'
>
> She got the job!

So there are four online strengths assessments that assess what we have defined as a strength: *an activity that you are good at*, and *that energises and motivates you* and *gives you great results*. The four are:

1. Realise2©
2. Strengthscope™
3. StrengthsFinder™
4. VIA (Values In Action).

You might have come across other tools for assessing strengths, such as the Strengths Deployment Inventory (SDI), which define strengths in a slightly different way. Since we believe that the energising element of a strength is so important, we have chosen the four above to focus more specifically on.

As you will see, these four all have their own vocabulary for the labels they use for each strength. Some of the words come from US English (Strengthsfinder™), for example 'Woo', rather than UK English. They also have differing total numbers of strengths.

The four online strengths assessments and their menus of strengths:

Realise2© (60 strengths)		Strengthscope™ (24 strengths)	Strengthsfinder™ (34 strengths)	VIA (Values In Action) (24 strengths)
Action	Incubator	Collaboration	Achiever	Creativity
Adherence	Innovation	Common Sense	Activator	Curiosity
Adventure	Judgement	Compassion	Adaptability	Open-Mindedness
Authenticity	Legacy	Courage	Analytical	Love of Learning
Bounceback	Listener	Creativity	Arranger	Perspective
Catalyst	Mission	Critical Thinking	Belief	Bravery
Centred	Moral Compass	Decisiveness	Command	Persistence
Change Agent	Narrator	Detail Orientation	Communication	Integrity
Compassion	Optimism	Developing Others	Competition	Vitality

▶

Realise2© (60 strengths)		Strengthscope™ (24 strengths)	Strengthsfinder™ (34 strengths)	VIA (Values In Action) (24 strengths)
Competitive	Order	Efficiency	Connectedness	Love
Connector	Persistence	Emotional Control	Consistency	Kindness
Counterpoint	Personal Responsibility	Empathy	Context	Social Intelligence
Courage	Personalisation	Enthusiasm	Deliberative	Citizenship
Creativity	Persuasion	Flexibility	Developer	Fairness
Curiosity	Planful	Initiative	Discipline	Leadership
Detail	Prevention	Leading	Empathy	Forgiveness and Mercy
Drive	Pride	Optimism	Focus	Humility and Modesty
Efficacy	Rapport Builder	Persuasiveness	Futuristic	Prudence
Emotional Awareness	Reconfiguration	Relationship Building	Harmony	Self-Regulation
Empathic Connection	Relationship Deepener	Resilience	Ideation	Appreciation of Beauty and Excellence
Enabler	Resilience	Results Focus	Includer	Gratitude
Equality	Resolver	Self-Confidence	Individualisation	Hope
Esteem Builder	Scribe	Self-Improvement	Input	Humour
Explainer	Self-Awareness	Strategic Mindedness	Intellection	Spirituality
Feedback	Service		Learner	
Gratitude	Spotlight		Maximiser	
Growth	Strategic Awareness		Positivity	
Humility	Time Optimiser		Relator	
Humour	Unconditionality		Responsibility	
Improver	Work Ethic		Restorative	
			Self-Assurance	
			Significance	
			Strategic	
			Woo	

As far as we are concerned, each product has its own advantages and disadvantages, and which one suits you best may depend on your context and your individual preference.

The next table aims to give you an overview of what you get with each model, and their similarities and differences.

	Realise2©	Strengthscope™	Strengthsfinder™	VIA (Values In Action)
Country of HQ	UK	UK	USA	USA
Number of strengths	60	24	34	24
Instant public online access	Yes	No (only by arrangement)	Yes	Yes
Broad focus/ Work focus	Broad	Work	Work	Broad
Can include online 360 degree feedback	No	Yes	No	No
Includes weaknesses too	Yes	Yes (lower scoring strengths)	Yes (in full report version)	Yes (called bottom strengths)
Can provide team report	Yes	Yes	No	Yes (Pro Version)
How does it subdivide the strengths into categories?	▮ Thinking ▮ Being ▮ Relating ▮ Communicating ▮ Motivating	▮ Thinking ▮ Emotional ▮ Relational ▮ Execution	▮ Strategic Thinking ▮ Influencing ▮ Relationship-Building ▮ Executing	▮ Wisdom and Knowledge ▮ Courage ▮ Humanity ▮ Justice ▮ Temperance ▮ Transcendence
Costs (April 2014)	Standard profile £16 + VAT. Premium profile £30 + VAT.	Standard profile £35 + VAT. 360 degree feedback version £50 + VAT.	Top 5 strengths report $9.99. Full report $89.	Standard profile report FREE. VIA Me! report $20. VIA Pro report $40

The table could help guide your thinking about which online assessment to use for yourself, and also which you might want your team to take.

Other factors may influence your decision about which model to use. You may have a competency framework in your organisation and wonder how your existing set-up can be used to measure strengths. We have worked with organisations to devise processes that allow them to continue with their own systems and to have strengths assessments working alongside them. See more on this later, on strengths-focused performance appraisals (in Chapter 12). We don't recommend one particular model of those explained on the last few pages. You will be able to find out which one would work best for your own organisation.

Your choice may also be determined by whether you are doing your self-assessment completely on your own, or whether you are in a situation where others around you in a team or organisation are already using a particular model. You may also be working with a coach who favours one of these models or is qualified to debrief the assessment for one or more. Either way, we are sure you'll find any conversation about your strengths interesting, energising and enlightening.

Now that we've looked at the variety of ways you can assess your strengths we'll go on to look at how you can best develop them.

ACTION POINTS

Identifying My own strengths

1. Use one or more of our five methods to get very familiar with your strengths, untapped strengths, overplayed strengths, learned behaviours and weaknesses.

2. Look for opportunities to use your strengths more.

3. Consider how significant your weaknesses are to your performance.

4. Go on and work with the development tools (in Chapter 4). These will show you how to optimise your development.

Developing **M**y strengths and managing **M**y weaknesses

Success is achieved by developing our strengths,
not by eliminating our weaknesses.
(Marilyn Vos Savant, writer)

WHEN YOU KNOW WHAT your strengths are, you need to go on to use them *and* develop them if you want to have more energy in your work, feel more motivated and achieve an even higher level of performance. As a leader, you will undoubtedly invest time thinking about how you can continuously improve your leadership effectiveness. Focusing on developing your strengths and managing only those significant weaknesses that are critical for your role is a fast way to improving your effectiveness.

As you go on to identify strengths to develop, you may be curious about whether these are the 'right' strengths for a leader to have. This is an important question and in this chapter we will also take a look at some of the evidence to support the different theories about what great leadership looks like, and the key strengths behind it.

By the end of this chapter you will have answers to the following questions:

1. Why develop my strengths?
2. How can I develop my strengths?
3. Why manage my weaknesses and how can I do it?
4. How can I use the R5 Action Plan to develop my strengths and manage my weaknesses?
5. What are the strengths of great leaders?

Why develop my strengths?

Here's a reminder of the good reasons for developing your strengths as a leader, which are:

▌ you will gain more satisfaction from your work – increased energy and motivation;

▌ you will have a route for reaching even higher levels of performance in the most enjoyable way;

▌ your leadership strengths will have even more impact;

▌ you will improve the perception others have of your leadership effectiveness;

▌ you can invest your time and energy developing in areas that really make a difference.

How can I develop my strengths?

If you have identified your strengths using one of the methods outlined in the previous chapter, you will be ready to think about how you can actively develop these strengths so that they make a real difference to you and your leadership effectiveness. It is wise to focus on developing just a few strengths at a time, perhaps between three and five, and also to make sure they are the most important strengths for you to develop. These strengths can then become your significant strengths, which are strengths that make you stand out and contribute to your effectiveness as a leader.[1]

Choosing the 'right' strengths to develop

In order that you select the 'right' strengths for development it is good to consider the following questions:

▌ Are you already good at this? Do others agree?

▌ Does the thought of using this strength more really enthuse and motivate you?

▌ Does your role, your team or your organisation need this strength?

▌ Will using this strength have a positive impact on you, your goals, other people or the organisation?

---

[1]   Zenger, J. H., et al. (2012) *How to Be Exceptional: Drive leadership success by magnifying your strengths,* New York, McGraw-Hill.

If the answer to all the above questions is 'Yes' then you have a perfect opportunity to do some strengths development and explore the many different ways you can do this. Take a minute now to note the strengths you would like to focus on developing.

Exercise

What 3–5 strengths would I like to develop?

Eight ways to develop strengths

Developing a strength is not just about using it more often. Doing even more of what is working is certainly one option, but it might not always be what is needed. Remember that strengths overplayed can become a weakness. Others might think you are already applying this strength in the right quantity at the right times and in the right situations.

When you have selected the strengths you want to develop, this is a time to be creative and consider all the different options available to you and to select options that will have most benefit to you, your team and your organisation. The options that we will explore are:

1. Test the limits of your area of strength.
2. Ask others for feedback, ideas and suggestions.
3. Learn new skills or take on new tasks that will provide opportunities to apply the strength.
4. Practise and develop strengths that are complementary (cross-training).
5. Coach, or train others.
6. Learn to regulate strengths overplayed.
7. Incorporate strengths development into your development plan.
8. Find yourself a coach or mentor.

Test the limits of your area of strength

If you have done the exercise above and identified three to five strengths that you would like to develop, you can look at each one in turn. Ask yourself how you can stretch the limits of how you are applying the strength to see whether you can achieve an even higher level of competence, performance and fulfilment. It might be a simple matter of doing more of what is working in a given context, whilst checking that the strength does not become overplayed.

However, if high levels of performance are already being achieved, there might not be much scope left for further improvement. Doing more of what is already working in the same context often does not make all that much difference to levels of satisfaction and performance. So, another way to stretch the limits of a strength is to find ways to apply it in a different context.

In the real world . . .

Previously (in Chapter 3) we introduced an example of Mary and explored her many strengths. One of her strengths was Relationship Builder and this was the one that she chose to develop, realising that she could find different ways of applying this strength. She identified an opportunity to push for an even higher level of competence in this strength by setting herself a target of establishing links with the Directors with whom she hadn't previously built strong relationships. Although this was a challenge, it was one that she relished and, as you can no doubt imagine, stretching the limits of her strength in this way had several other payoff benefits for Mary.

So, try this yourself and answer the following questions to capture some initial ideas for things you can do to test the limits of your strengths that you want to develop.

Exercise

Which strengths would you like to test the limits of?

What ideas have you got for doing this?

In what other contexts could you use these strengths?

Ask others for feedback, ideas and suggestions

There is huge value to be had in seeking feedback from others on how they see you applying your strengths and the impact it has had. However, whilst feedback has value, you cannot go back and change what you have done in the past, so it can be much more useful to get ideas and suggestions from people about what you can do in the future in order to utilise your strengths.

Marshall Goldsmith[2] developed the very effective process of Feedforward. This involves selecting a small number of trusted colleagues and saying to each of them: 'I am working on developing a strength of mine (name the strength). Can you give me two or three ideas for what I could do to

---

2   Goldsmith, M. *FeedForward*. www.marshallgoldsmithfeedforward.com Accessed 21.7.14.

use this strength even more effectively?' You then note the ideas, thank your colleague, and go on to the next colleague. You decide what you want to do from the long list of undoubtedly very useful suggestions. The process continues with you going back regularly to ask for feedback on how you are doing and ask for further suggestions.

> **In the real world . . .**
>
> In our example, Mary decided to take this approach to help her understand how best she could apply her strength of Creativity. Her colleagues gave several suggestions, including encouraging her to share more readily her ideas at meetings, even if they weren't fully formed. They also suggested that she could get involved in some Think Tanks that were about to happen within the organisation. One of the most useful suggestions that she was given was to consider using her interest in creative thinking to help others explore and develop their ideas, rather than always being the one putting forward ideas.

Once again, try this yourself and answer the following questions.

> **Exercise**
>
> About which strengths would you like to get feedback from others?
>
> About which strengths would you like to get Feedforward suggestions?
>
> Who will you ask?
>
> How often will you ask, in order to check progress?

Learn new skills or take on new tasks that will provide opportunities to apply the strength

You can develop a strength by finding opportunities to learn a new skill or take on a new task that will give you scope to practise and stretch your existing strength. For example, if you have a strength in Analytical Thinking, what other duties could you take on that would help your department and your organisation at the same time as giving you the opportunity to do something you love and also allowing you to develop your strength?

You might identify an untapped strength that you do not get enough opportunity to use in work. If it is possible to find a way of utilising this strength at work in a way that is of benefit to your role and organisation, then this is an ideal outcome. However, sometimes that strength is just not needed, or at least, developing the strength to be a significant strength is not going to make a huge difference to your effectiveness as a leader.

Not being able to use a strength can have a dampening effect on your motivation – it feels like something is missing or that your needs are not being met. In these situations, what can work well is finding a way of applying the strength to a new skill or task outside of work. In that way, the need to use the strength is met, and energy from doing so is derived outside of the workplace, leading to a very positive feeling towards work–life balance. You may also want to consider what this says about your current job and your future career options.

So, here are some questions for you to consider in order to identify some actions you can take.

Exercise

What new skills could you learn in order to develop your strengths?

What new tasks could you take on that would allow you to develop your strengths?

What could you do outside of work that will allow you to develop and play to your strengths in a way that would not be appropriate or possible at work?

Practise and develop strengths that are complementary (cross-training)

Zenger, Folkman and colleagues[3] have recently discovered something very interesting in relation to strengths: that in many instances 'cross-training' can have a far more powerful impact on the development of a strength than the more 'linear' route to development we are used to, i.e. finding ways to apply the strength more. To illustrate their idea, I (Kathy) was training to prepare myself for a challenging trek in the Andes. Part of my training involved a few walking weekends in the UK, but this was only one option available to me. I realised that my walking practice needed to be supported by compatible activities, such as swimming to maintain stamina and support my joints, running to build my aerobic capacity and so on. All this 'cross-training' had a noticeable impact on my ability to complete my trek much more successfully than if I had only practised my walking skills!

Taking the cross-training approach, when you have a strength that you want to develop further so that you can really maximise its potential, you

3   Zenger, J. H., et al. (2012) *How to Be Exceptional: Drive leadership success by magnifying your strengths*, New York, McGraw-Hill.

can think about which of your other strengths might be complementary to it. The idea is that when you apply this complementary strength to the strength you want to develop, then you really get the chance to stand out for this strength.

> ### In the real world . . .
>
> We will give you an example of this in practice. Mary decided that she would like to develop her strength of Relationship Builder, because she realised that this was paying dividends for her at work. She struggled to think of many more ways she could build more relationships per se, beyond what she was already doing, and her idea, mentioned earlier, to build relationships with the directors she didn't know so well. However, when her coach challenged her to think of related strengths that she could work on, which were complementary to Relationship Builder, the path became clearer. Mary decided to focus on the competency of Developer (an untapped strength) because of the fact that many of the activities that are involved in developing others require a good rapport and good working relationships to be built. She decided to be more meticulous with her mid-year review conversations with her team members, spending more time discussing their personal and career development and listening to their needs. She also offered to facilitate some short training sessions as part of induction training offered to those new to the organisation, which also gave her the opportunity to build early relationships with these people. So, both of these activities, although they were fundamentally about the strength of Developer, allowed her to further develop her strength of Relationship Builder.

Now it's your turn to think about how this could work for you.

> ### Exercise
>
> Which strength(s) might be complementary to the strength(s) you want to develop?
>
> What could you do to develop in these complementary strength(s)?

Coach or train others

An effective way to develop a strength is to teach, train or coach somebody else to be good at that strength. When we want to train others, we have to pay attention to what we ourselves are doing when we are doing things right, so that we can show others how to do it well. When we train other people it heightens our understanding of an area of competence, such that we become more of an expert.

> **In the real world . . .**
>
> Going back to our case study example, Mary was perceived by others to be a role model in the way she networked and built relationships with others. This had a positive impact on her peers and also internal and external customers. New managers within the Scientific Projects department were frequently directed to spend time with Mary as part of their induction so that they could learn from her about how to build an effective network quickly. By acting as a coach, Mary became more aware of her own behaviour and where she could become even more effective.

What about you?

> **Exercise**
>
> Which strength(s) could you develop by training or coaching others?
>
> What could you do? Who could you train or coach?

Learn to regulate strengths overplayed

We have talked already about ensuring that in the process of developing your strengths, they do not go into overdrive. If a strength is overplayed, there is a risk that it can become a weakness. For example, a weakness of being too laissez faire might be the strength of Flexibility being overplayed.

A good way to manage your strengths and prevent them being overplayed is to know what a strength being overplayed would look like, and constantly maintain a high enough level of self-awareness to notice when you have reached this point and when you need to pull back a little. You can then do what is needed to regulate this overplayed strength.

An even better way to find out whether we have any strengths that are overplayed is to get feedback from others. For those who would welcome this, some of the strengths assessment tools referred to previously (in Chapter 3) enable you to get feedback from others on your perceived strengths. But you will recall that you don't need a formal strengths assessment to ask people for their ideas on what you can do differently. If you have a strength overplayed and you approach people with a genuine intention to learn from their feedback and suggestions, you will probably find out about it from them. Your team or your line manager may be the best placed and most motivated to give you this feedback. After all, any changes you make will be to their advantage!

Take a few minutes to answer the next questions.

Exercise

Which of your strengths might you be overplaying, and in which situations?

If you were overplaying one of your strengths, what would that look like?

Does this happen? If so, what can you do to regulate this strength?

Incorporate strengths development into your development plan

Many organisations' performance management processes include ensuring that employees have development goals as part of a development plan. When you have identified strengths that you want to develop, it is a very good idea to incorporate your ideas for developing these strengths into your overall Development Plan and your development objectives. See the next chapter (Chapter 5) for more on how you can create strengths-focused development objectives for yourself. (Refer to Chapter 13 for how you can help others do this and also how to have strengths-focused development discussions with your direct reports.)

Find yourself a coach or mentor

One final means of developing your strengths is to find yourself a coach or mentor to help you do this. It might be that your own line manager is willing to offer you some coaching support to help you develop a plan for maximising the potential of your strengths. Alternatively, you might want to look outside of the organisation for this type of support for a specified period of time (usually up to six months) and select for yourself an executive coach who adopts a strengths-focused approach. There is much value to be had from working with a coach from outside the organisation who can offer a range of coaching approaches to support you and will ensure that you do your own best thinking, as opposed to giving you advice on what you should do.

Another option is to request a mentor, who is likely to come from within the organisation. Good mentors will tend to take a coaching approach, supporting you in generating your own best thinking and working to your agenda (developing your strengths), but they also bring the value of their wisdom and experience, which can be helpful. One question that people often ask is: 'Do I choose a mentor who has similar strengths to me and who I can model, or do I choose someone who is very different who might challenge my thinking?' There is no definite answer to this and it is a matter of individual preference. As long as your mentor is clear that you want them to help you develop your strengths and manage any significant weaknesses, then a good mentoring relationship is invariably something that is of real value to both parties.

Why manage my weaknesses and how can I do it?

We've talked a lot about how to develop your strengths, and quite rightly so, because the evidence suggests that this is where you should focus your attention to get the best results.

However, that is not to say that you shouldn't focus on weaknesses at all. We have previously mentioned that when you have identified a weakness, the first thing to ask yourself is: 'Is it important?' If the answer is 'Yes' then there is a definite need to begin to manage the weakness and eliminate any possible negative impact. If you have a significant weakness that is a potential derailer for you, the evidence suggests that you should fix it immediately.[4]

Identifying weaknesses to work on

So how do you know which weaknesses you need to work on? You might discover a weakness in one of several ways: your manager might point it out to you; you might have received 360 degree feedback that indicates a weakness; you might have completed your 5 Steps Strength Map (in Chapter 3); or you might be so self-aware that you realise your shortcomings. We have previously mentioned that most people are keener to notice their own faults before they notice their strengths.

When you discover a weakness, there are certain questions to ask yourself before committing to pay attention to it from a development perspective:

▌ Does it matter to me? Is my performance being affected by this weakness?

▌ Does it matter to others? Is this weakness impacting others' ability to perform at their best?

▌ Is this weaker competence important in my role and to my organisation?

▌ Is this weakness a potential derailer for me?

---

4   Zenger, J. H., et al. (2012) *How to Be Exceptional: Drive leadership success by magnifying your strengths*, New York, McGraw-Hill.

If the answer is 'Yes' to any of the above questions, then there definitely is a need to manage this as a significant weakness. This is arguably where you should start with your development because if your weakness is critical for your leadership effectiveness and performance, no matter what your other strengths are, you will struggle to be fully effective if you don't address the weakness.

Six ways to manage your weaknesses

So how do you manage your weaknesses in a strengths-focused way? Well, there are several approaches available to you:

1. Seek feedback and suggestions from others.
2. Find a role model.
3. Practise to make it 'good enough'.
4. Draw on your strengths to manage the weaknesses.
5. Build the management of your weaknesses into your development plan.
6. Complementary role sharing.

Seek feedback and suggestions from others

In the same way that you gather feedback and suggestions from others about how you might play more to your strengths, you can also ask key stakeholders for suggestions about how you can respond to and manage your weaknesses.

You will need to be clear with your stakeholders which weakness you are particularly interested in addressing. It can be helpful for you to hear their feedback about behaviours they have noticed you demonstrate in relation to the weakness and the impact these behaviours have had. What can be more useful, however, is to ask for Feedforward suggestions from them on what they would like to see you do differently. You don't have to do everything that is suggested to you, but we are sure that you will get some pretty useful suggestions.

As a reminder, you simply ask this question: 'I'm looking at developing my competence of ... Can you give me one or two suggestions for how I can demonstrate this competence more effectively?' You don't even have to tell them it is a weakness!

Take some time to answer the next questions.

Exercise

Which weaker areas would you like to pay attention to?

From which stakeholders would you value some feedback and suggestions?

Having asked them, what suggestions have they given you?

Which of their suggestions do you now want to act on?

Find a role model

Many of us learn best by observing others. If you have a weakness that you want to overcome, can you think of anyone who demonstrates this behaviour well – someone who has this as a strength? By carefully observing what they do, and even asking them about what they think and feel whilst practising the strength, you can find ideas for modelling the behaviour.

Here are some questions for you to think about, which will help you clarify what practising this strength is about.

Exercise

Which weaker area would you like to pay attention to?

Who do you know who has this as a strength?

What do you see them do?

Having spoken to them, what have you found out about what drives their behaviour? For example, what do they value, what do they believe, what do they think and feel before they demonstrate the strength?

What have you learnt?

What can you do to try out some new behaviours?

We mentioned that one way of developing your strengths is to find yourself a coach or mentor. This is clearly also an option for helping you address any significant weaknesses. If you select a mentor who has a strength in the area where you have a weakness, this is an ideal opportunity for you to have regular access to somebody who you can model and who can help you explore some different ideas for turning round your weaknesses.

Practise to make it 'good enough'

When you have decided what you can do to address your weakness and you have developed an action plan, continually monitor the impact of the changes you make to your behaviour. Notice what works for you and for others, and continue to do that, until the behaviour becomes a habit and is no longer a problem.

If something has previously been a significant weakness, it is very unlikely that it will ever become a significant strength – so you may not want to try to make it so. It is more likely to become a learned behaviour. When you have made enough changes that have become ingrained as part of the way you now do things, you have done enough. There is no need to force yourself to become perfect in something that probably doesn't give you much energy and motivation.

Here are the questions to consider and begin to create an action plan.

Exercise

What new behaviours will you put into place to manage your significant weakness(es)?

How will you monitor and measure the impact of these changes?

How can you get further feedback from others to ensure that any changes you make are having a positive effect?

How will you know when you are 'good enough'?

Draw on your strengths to manage the weakness

A clever way of managing a weakness is to find some of your own strengths to call upon to help you manage the weakness. In this way, something that was previously perceived as a potential energy drain for you can suddenly seem a lot more appealing.

In the real world . . .

To go back to our example, Mary wasn't as perfect as we might have made out! Her 360 degree feedback and subsequent discussions highlighted a weakness in dealing with confrontation and conflict in an empathic way. The feedback suggested that when she got into conflict she became very results focused and overly directive, sharing her own views very forcefully. In these situations she was seen as lacking empathy and being unwilling to listen to others' views. However, Mary also liked to keep harmony in a team and she didn't like to upset people. When she realised that her inability to deal with others empathically in times of conflict was preventing her having the open conversations that she needed to, she realised she had to do something about it. She was able to see how she could use her strength of Relationship Builder to prepare relationships to be able to withstand healthy disagreement. She also realised that she could use her strength of Creativity to see disagreements as an opportunity to be creative with others and look on diverse views as a means of generating new and different ideas.

Now it's your turn again.

Exercise

Which weakness would you like to manage?

Which strengths might you be able to call on to help you manage this weakness?

What can you do?

What impact will this have?

Build the management of your weaknesses into your development plan

As with strengths, it is a good idea to address any limiting weakness by setting yourself a clear development objective with a motivating and compelling action plan. Once again, we explain how you can do this for yourself (in Chapter 5), and (in Chapter 13) we look at how you can support others in creating a motivational development plan that addresses both strengths and weaknesses.

Complementary strengths role sharing

We have previously pointed out that it can be very draining if you regularly have to exercise behaviours that are weaknesses for you. After all, weaknesses are things that you don't like doing, that don't energise you, and that generally lead to poorer results. If the behaviour in question is critical to your role, a smarter way of managing your weakness is to find a colleague who has the behaviour as a strength. By analysing your relative strengths, you can between you find a way of managing your workload in a way that maximises each person's opportunities to play to their strengths and minimises the need to play to your weaknesses.

To give you an example, Mary had a weakness of Communicator and she would often notice that people in her team appeared confused when she presented information. She would occasionally appear irritated by this. Mary discovered that someone in her team, Ian, loved making information clear to others. She was very pleased when Ian very willingly agreed to support her by taking over responsibility for preparing certain presentations for her, and even conducted the presentation himself at times. This also gave Mary an opportunity to learn from Ian and it gave Ian a chance to develop himself at the same time as playing to his strengths. A great outcome!

What about you?

Exercise

With which of your colleagues whom you work closely with might there be an opportunity to role share in a way that complements your strengths?

What strengths does that person have?

Which of their strengths complements your weakness?

How might you divide up your work in a way that maximises the opportunity for your colleague to play to their strengths and minimises the need for you to use your weakness?

How can I use the R5 Action Plan to develop my strengths and manage my weaknesses?

Previously (in Chapter 3) we introduced the 5 Step Strengths Map and you may have taken the opportunity to complete it. When you have completed your 5 Step Strengths Map and created a clearer picture of your strengths, your untapped strengths, your learned behaviours, your strengths overplayed and your weaknesses, you can begin to ask yourself specific questions that will enable you to identify some ideas and actions for developing your strengths and managing your weaknesses.

Quite simply, you will need to consider what you would like to do in relation to each of the five areas of your strengths map. To help you with this, you can complete an R5 Action Plan.

Completing your R5 Action Plan

Each of the five areas within the 5 Step Strengths Map requires a different type of action. The R5 Action Plan covers each of the five areas, asking you specific questions to help you identify some useful actions to build your strengths and manage your weaknesses. The action plan will enable you to:

1 **R**eap your strengths.

2 **R**elease the potential of your untapped strengths.

3 **R**egulate the strengths that you overplay.

4 **R**educe the amount of time you have to use your learned behaviours.

5 **R**espond to important weaknesses.

Before you have a go at completing your own plan, here's a reminder of the 5 Step Strengths Map, along with the questions you can ask yourself to identify some actions to put into a plan to develop your strengths.

1. Your **strengths** – the things you are good at that you energise you. You'll want to make the most of these.	**REAP – your strengths** What can you do to use these strengths more? What sort of work, objectives or activities would help you use your strengths more?
2. Your **untapped strengths** – the strengths that you don't use as much as you would want to. These are an area of huge potential for you.	**RELEASE – your untapped strengths** What can you do to create opportunities to use these strengths more and release this potential?
3. Your **strengths overplayed**. If there are times when you use a strength too much or in an inappropriate context, such that it is having a negative impact, we call this a 'strength overplayed'. You'll want to focus on using the right strength, in the right amount, in the right situation.	**REGULATE – your strengths overplayed** What can you do to regulate any strengths that you use too much?
4. Your **learned behaviours** – the things you do well that don't energise you, and that drain you. You'll want to reduce the amount of time that these occupy you.	**REDUCE – your learned behaviours** What can you do to reduce and minimise the use of these things you do well but don't really enjoy?

▶

5. Your **weaknesses** – the things you don't perform well and that drain you when you do them. You'll want to be clear about how best to respond to these, particularly if they are critical to your work-based goals.	RESPOND – to your weaknesses Are these behaviours important in your role? If so, what can you do to develop them – or call on other strengths to help you? How can you make your weaknesses irrelevant? Or, how can you manage them?

Exercise: Your R5 Action Plan to develop your strengths

Use the R5 Action Plan to capture your responses to the questions and begin to identify opportunities to develop your strengths and manage your learned behaviours and weaknesses.

Steps 1–3: The activities that energise you

1. Your strengths REAP What can you do to use these strengths more? What sort of work, objectives or activities would help you use your strengths more?	**2. Your untapped strengths – RELEASE** What can you do to create opportunities to use these strengths more and release this potential?	**3. Your overplayed strengths – REGULATE** What can you do to regulate any strengths that you use too much?

Steps 4–5: The activities that drain your energy

4. Your learned behaviours – REDUCE What can you do to reduce and minimise the use of these things you do well but don't really enjoy?	**5. Your weaknesses – RESPOND** Are these behaviours important in your role? If so, what can you do to develop them – or call on other strengths to help you? How can you make your weakness irrelevant? Or manage them?

What are the strengths of great leaders?

If you've mapped your own strengths and created a development plan for them, you might be wondering how your strengths compare to what are considered to be the strengths of effective leaders.

There is a huge amount of information available about the qualities of a great leader. With a wide variety of theories on leadership, no one can hope to have the final word on the subject, but there is some evidence to support the different theories about what great leadership looks like and, also, the key strengths behind it.

Over the last twenty or thirty years a number of writers have given us some very useful models of leadership based on robust research. Let's look at a few.

Kouzes and Posner[5]

Back in 1987, in their seminal work *The Leadership Challenge*, these authors laid out the five leadership practices that their research had shown effective leaders do. The research was the analysis of hundreds of interviews and hundreds of case studies and survey questionnaires.

The five practices are:

1. **Model the way.** Establishing and role modelling the principles concerning the way people should be treated and the way goals should be pursued.

2. **Inspire a shared vision.** Creating a passionate vision of the future, an ideal and unique image of what the organisation can become.

3. **Challenge the process.** Continually searching for opportunities to change the status quo and to find innovative ways to improve the organisation.

4. **Enable others to act.** Fostering collaboration and involvement and building spirited teams.

5. **Encourage the heart.** Building engagement and celebrating success and contribution.

Zenger and Folkman[6]

In 2001, based on analysis of the evidence from 200,000 assessments of 20,000 managers, these authors suggested that the best leaders had 16 competencies in five areas.

---

[5] Kouzes, J. M. and Posner, B. Z. (2002) *The Leadership Challenge* (3rd edn), San Francisco: Jossey-Bass.

[6] Zenger, J. H. and Folkman, J. (2009) *The Extraordinary Leader: Turning good managers into great leaders*, New York, McGraw-Hill Professional.

Getting results	Leading change	Character	Interpersonal skills	Personal capability
Focuses on results	Develops strategic perspective	Displays honesty and integrity	Inspires and motivates others	Exhibits technical/ professional expertise
Establishes stretch goals	Champions change		Communicates powerfully and broadly	Solves problems and analyses issues
Takes initiative	Connects the group to the outside world		Builds relationships	Innovates
			Develops others	Practises self-development
			Collaborates and fosters team work	

They found that competent leaders would have a significant strength in at least one of the 16 competencies, and that their competence as a leader increased as another significant competency appeared. Those judged to be great leaders were those whose assessments judged them to have between three and five 'profound' strengths. Interestingly it transpires that having more than five profound strengths from the 16 does not seem to increase the perceptions of others about your effectiveness as a leader.

Further study of these 16 competencies in the last few years has led Zenger, Folkman and colleagues to suggest that the strongest correlation to success lies with this subset of five competencies, ranked in order of importance (they are shaded in the table above):

1. Inspires and motivates others to high performance.
2. Communicates powerfully and broadly.
3. Establishes stretch goals.
4. Develops strategic perspective.
5. Solves problems and analyses issues.

Zenger, Folkman and their colleagues went on to do very interesting work[7] showing that leaders improved their effectiveness more by focusing on

---

[7] Zenger, J. H., et al. (2012) *How to Be Exceptional: Drive leadership success by magnifying your strengths,* New York, McGraw-Hill.

building strengths. In the same work they also presented evidence to show the value of 'cross-training' referred to earlier in this chapter.

Rath and Conchie

In 2008, two writers from Gallup,[8] Rath and Conchie, presented their leadership research based on the StrengthsFinder™ strengths assessment model that we outlined previously (in Chapter 3). They surveyed a million work teams, conducted more than 50,000 in-depth interviews with leaders, and even interviewed 20,000 followers around the world to ask exactly why they followed the most important leader in their life.

Rath and Conchie found that the most effective leaders were not necessarily 'well-rounded', but they did create teams that covered the strengths they did not themselves possess. The research showed that successful teams have strengths in four broad domains:

1. Strategic thinking
2. Relationship building
3. Influencing
4. Execution.

The successful leaders they studied had a significant strength in one or more of these domains (but usually not all of them) and then ensured that they had people around them with strengths in the other domains. This fits very much with the notion of complementary role sharing that we mentioned earlier as a way of developing your strengths.

How do your strengths relate to this?

As you can see, even when the studies are based on a huge amount of research, the analysis of that research yields slightly different results. The leadership cake can be cut in different ways.

However, there seem to be common themes across all three models and these are the ability to:

▌ think strategically, to create a clear and compelling vision of the future;

▌ communicate that vision in a way that inspires and motivates people to do what needs doing;

---

[8] Rath, T. and Conchie, B. (2008) *Strengths Based Leadership: Great leaders, teams, and why people follow*, New York, Gallup Press.

▌ create engagement and strong relationships;

▌ get things done;

▌ change and improve, and to solve problems.

Considering all these points, if you want to be an effective leader you should identify a significant strength in at least one of these five themes. For those you may not be so strong in, consider how others in your team could provide these. And remember, our definition of strength is not just about competencies you are good at, it is also about activities that you love to do.

ACTION POINTS

Developing **My** strengths and managing **My** weaknesses

1 Choose three to five strengths that you would like to develop and stand out for.

2 Create a strategy for developing these strengths and identify some actions you want to take (use the R5 Action Plan).

3 Notice the impact on your energy and performance as you work on developing these strengths.

4 Identify any significant weaknesses that need to be addressed.

5 Create a strategy for responding to the area(s) of weakness (use the R5 Action Plan).

6 Notice the impact on your performance as you work on improving the weakness.

Aligning **My** goals and objectives with **My** strengths

There is no passion to be found playing small – in settling for a life that is less than the one you are capable of living.
(Nelson Mandela)

IN MOST ORGANISATIONS, performance management processes have been established for some time where the goals of the organisation are cascaded down the different levels. It makes sense for you to have clarity about what is expected of you at work and also know how your contribution leads to the success of the organisation as a whole. It is also important that you are given the opportunity to identify what and how you need to develop in order to perform at your best.

Whilst this process is invaluable, it is unfortunately often viewed as a tedious task. Introducing a strength focus to the process adds a totally different quality to the discussions and the resulting plans are much more meaningful and motivational.

You may by now have generated many ideas for developing your strengths, and you will now be ready to think about how you can develop some motivational goals and objectives that are aligned with your strengths.

By the end of this chapter you will have answers to the following questions:

1. Why align my goals and objectives with my strengths?
2. Which goals and objectives can I align with my strengths?
3. How do I create strengths-focused business objectives?
4. How do I create strengths-focused development objectives?

Why align my goals and objectives with my strengths?

You may well have been through the objective-setting process many times in your career and therefore be very familiar with it. Have you considered the potential to enhance your own level of performance if you were to ensure that each of your goals is aligned with your strengths?

If you have read this far, we are sure you'll be able to recite the many benefits of aligning your goals with your strengths, but just to recap, it is likely to lead to these outcomes:

▌ goals and objectives will be achieved much faster and more easily;

▌ working on your goals and objectives will be energising, motivating and fun;

▌ a greater sense of authenticity – not just going through the motions, but working on things that are aligned with who you are;

▌ a higher level of output and performance.

Which goals and objectives can I align with my strengths?

It might be that you are a very goal-focused person and you have a whole list of goals and objectives that you are now ready to align with your strengths. For some, however, having goals might be a new concept. There are three main types of goals that you might have in work that you can align with your strengths.

Three types of goals

1 **Business goals and objectives.** It might be that you are self-employed and set your own business goals for the year for a given time period. For those employed in an organisation, your business goals and objectives will be those that you agreed with your line manager when the annual performance review cycle started. We wonder, are these discussions positive experiences where possibilities are explored with energy and enthusiasm, or does it just feel like going through the motions? Let's hope it's the former.

2 **Development goals and objectives.** If you are working in an organisation where you have some business goals, it is likely that you will also have had a development conversation with your line manager and you will have some development goals. These goals might have been informed by the review of last year's business objectives, by your new business objectives for the year or a result of a 360 degree feedback process. They might address development needs identified by looking at your organisation's competency framework, or your development goals might be to support your career needs. You may even have undertaken a strengths assessment and created some development goals from that. Especially if the latter is true, we hope that your goals do not all focus on improving weaknesses, but that they focus primarily on building strengths!

3 **Career goals.** Ideally you will have regular conversations with your line manager about your career plans. If not, it is easy to do some self-coaching and think about what you want to achieve in your career. You might consider over what period of time you want to achieve your goals, and what objectives and associated actions you need to set yourself to help you achieve those career plans. A strengths-focused approach to career planning suggests that you use your understanding of your strengths to help you plan a career that will be motivating, enjoyable, productive and fulfilling.

Whatever sort of goals you have in place, you can see the benefit of ensuring that they are aligned with your strengths.

How do I create strengths-focused business objectives?

You may already be familiar with the mnemonic and know that objectives should be **SMART**, but we think you can benefit from making sure all your objectives are **SMARTIE** ones! SMARTIE objectives are ones that are also **important** to you (as well as the organisation) and **energising** because they play directly to your strengths or because you have found ways to apply your strengths to help you achieve them.

So, all your objectives should be SMARTIE ones . . .

Specific and **S**trengths-focused

Measurable

Achievable

Relevant

Time-bound

Important

Energising

Unless you are lucky enough to have a line manager who has adopted the philosophy and behaviours of strengths-focused leaders, a good way to ensure that your business objectives are SMARTIE and are aligned with your strengths is to do some self-coaching using the following questions.

Setting business goals – questions to ask myself

Specific and strengths-focused

▍ What is my performance objective? What exactly needs to be achieved? What will success look like?

▍ How does this objective give me an opportunity to use my strengths? Which specific strengths does this objective play to?

▍ Which other strengths can I draw on to help me achieve this objective?

Measurable

▍ How will I measure my achievement of this objective? What will be tangible evidence of completion?

▍ How else?

Achievable

▍ How achievable is this goal?

▍ How will it stretch me?

Relevant

▍ How does this relate to my other goals, and the goals of my team?

Time-bound

▍ When does the objective need to be achieved?

▍ What are the milestones along the way?

Important

▎ What will be the positive impact on me, my job, my team and the organisation?

▎ What will be good about achieving this objective?

Energising

▎ On a scale of 1 to 10 (1 = lowest level, 10 = highest level), how enthusiastic do I feel about working towards this objective?

In the real world . . .

Here is an example of how Peter, a Regional Manager within a confectionery organisation, answered these questions.

Specific and strengths-focused

Q: What is my performance objective?

A: I need to ensure all my Area Managers successfully launch a 2 for 1 promotion on tins of chocolates within all convenience retail outlets, ready to start on November 1st.

Q: What exactly needs to be achieved?

A: As a result of the promotion, we aim to improve sales by 30 per cent during the month of the promotion (compared to the same month last year). This involves Area Managers influencing retailers to promote the product appropriately and ensuring stock is available to fulfil sales targets.

Q: What will success look like?

A: All Area Managers will have visited the convenience outlets in their area by the end of October. Sales meet or exceed 30 per cent increase compared to November last year.

Q: How does this objective give me an opportunity to use my strengths? Which specific strengths does this objective play to?

A: I can play to my strengths of Results Focus and Leadership. I can also play to my strength of Drive and competitiveness.

Q: Which other strengths can I draw on to help me achieve this objective?

A: I can also use my strength of Communicator to ensure that my team fully understand what is required. This strength will also help me in my liaison with the supply chain.

Measurable

Q: How will I measure my achievement of this objective? What will be a tangible evidence of completion?

A: The promotion will be launched in all stores on time and we will achieve the sales targets. I would also like to be the top-performing region in this promotion! Team morale will also be a good measure of success.

Achievable

Q: How achievable is this goal?

A: I believe we can do it. Customer demand is high at this time of year with Christmas on the horizon. The promotional graphics are great, too.

Q: How will it stretch me?

A: This will be a bit of challenge for me in terms of motivating and engaging my team of Area Managers, because this is a big 'ask' to get them to see all their customers within a month. I need to be careful to listen to their needs and not just be focused on results. That will be good for me to regulate this strength.

Relevant

Q: How does this relate to your other goals, and the goals of my team?

A: Well, my performance goals are all about increasing sales so this is really relevant. Success in this promotion will also help my team achieve the annual sales target.

Time-bound

Q: When does the objective need to be achieved?

A: Set-up needs to be achieved by the end of October. Sales increases need to be achieved week on week.

Q: What are the milestones along the way?

A: Firstly, I need to brief my team on what is required and get their ideas on how we can successfully launch the promotion. Then I will need to work with each Area Manager individually to establish a visit plan for their month. I also need to think about my sales forecasts and liaise with the supply chain to ensure adequate stock levels. I need to think about how I monitor sales each week and introduce some sort of fun competition within the team. I should also think about escorting some of the Area Managers on their visits, so that I can see what works and share best practice across the team. Whew! Quite a lot to be done!

Important

Q: What will be good about achieving this objective?

A: Success for the team and increased sales – it will be a great achievement.

Energising

Q: On a scale of 1 to 10 (1 = lowest level, 10 = highest level), how enthusiastic do I feel about working towards this objective?

A: 10 out of 10! I love being the best region in these sorts of promotions. It also gives my team a buzz when they are successful.

Here is the final version of Peter's objective:

'To successfully launch the tinned chocolates 2 for 1 promotion on 1st November in all convenience outlets, leading to year-on-year sales increase of 30 per cent for the month.'

 If you are the sort of person who likes to have a structure for your plans, you'll find a blank copy of a useful template in Appendix 1, and on our website at www.sfleadership.co.uk.

Here is an example of a completed template for Peter's business objective.

Objective	Measures of success	Strengths	Timing	Action plan
What is the objective?	How will you measure your achievement?	Which strengths are relevant to achieving this?	When is it to be achieved?	What actions will be taken to achieve the objective?
To successfully launch the tinned chocolates 2 for 1 promotion on 1st November in all convenience outlets, leading to year-on-year sales increase of 30% for the month.	All Area Managers will have visited the convenience outlets in their area by the end of October. Sales meet or exceed 30% increase compared to November last year.	Results Focus Leadership Drive Communicator	30 Nov 2014	1. Brief my team on requirements – get ideas on how we can successfully launch the promotion. 2. Meet with each Area Manager individually to establish a visit plan for their month. 3. Complete sales forecasts. 4. Liaise with supply chain to ensure adequate stock levels. 5. Create plan for how I monitor sales each week. 6. Devise a competition for the team. 7. Plan to escort some Area Managers on their visits, so that I can see what works. 8. Continue to share best practice across the team.

How do I create strengths-focused development objectives?

Well-constructed development objectives will ensure that you grow and develop in a way that positively impacts upon your performance, your strengths, your career plan and the business, too.

Identifying development goals

At the start of creating a development plan, it is a good idea to identify up to three development goals to work on at any one time. As a guide, at least two of these development goals build on strengths. To identify development goals to focus on, it can help to answer the following questions:

▌ What ideas for development have arisen from your discussions so far about your performance over the last year?

▌ What are some of the key strengths that you would like to build upon as part of your development plan?

▌ Are there any significant weaknesses that need managing?

▌ What development requirements have been discussed as being necessary to support the achievement of your objectives for the next period (skill, knowledge, behaviour or strengths)?

▌ What development requirements have been discussed in order for you to achieve your career aspirations?

When you have determined what to focus on in your development plan, you can use the SMARTIE framework to help you create a motivational strengths-focused objectives.

 There is a useful template for writing your development plan in Appendix 2, and on our website www.sfleadership.co.uk.

What about weaknesses?

You might be wondering how weaknesses should feature and be addressed in a development plan. We have already said that our inherent negativity bias as human beings constantly draws us to set goals that address our weaknesses, and we have shown you how that can have a very damaging effect on your performance if weaknesses are all you focus on. We have, however, pointed out that if there are any significant weaknesses that are potential derailers and that could really prevent you achieving outstanding performance, we are sure you will want to set some objectives to address these as part of your development planning. Just make sure that your development plan also includes areas of strength to build upon!

Three quick steps for 'strengthening' your development goals

In order to ensure that your development goals are aligned with your strengths, there are three things you can do:

1. Ensure that your development goals are related to building on strengths: unless there is significant weakness to address.

2. Use your strengths to manage your weaknesses: for every development goal that is addressing a weakness, consider what strengths you can bring to bear that will help you address the development need.

3. Spot the opportunity to play to your strengths in all your development goals: they will be more fun, more energising and much easier to achieve as a result.

ACTION POINTS

Aligning my goals and objectives with my strengths

1. If you already have business goals, go back and look at how you are playing to your strengths in the achievement of these goals. What more can you do to ensure that you are drawing on your strengths?

2. If you do not have business goals in place, use the template provided (Appendix 1) to design some SMARTIE goals that are aligned with your strengths.

3. If you already have some development goals, check how much these goals are focused on developing your strengths rather than your weaknesses. What can you do to make your development goals more focused on developing your strengths and only addressing significant weaknesses?

4. Use the template provided (Appendix 2) to design some new development goals that focus on developing your strengths and responding only to significant weaknesses.

Others' strengths

When well-being comes from engaging our strengths and virtues,
our lives are imbued with authenticity.
(Martin Seligman, psychologist, educator and author)

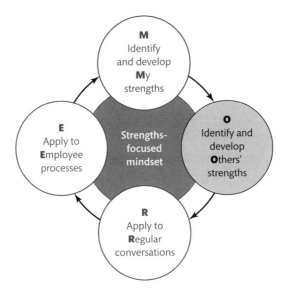

The '**O**' of the **MORE** model stands for 'Identify and Develop Other's strengths.

Having identified your own strengths and spent some time thinking about how you can build on and develop these strengths, you will be eager to support your team members in accessing the high levels of energy, engagement and performance that result from this.

Our aim in this section of the book is to give you a practical guide to how you can do this and where you might start. Rather than impose a strengths assessment on your team with no context, we offer you some ways that you might introduce a strengths focus to them so that they are actively involved in the decision. We then go on to outline the different ways that you can support your team members in identifying and developing their strengths and in managing any significant weakness.

So, in this section of the book we will cover:

1 Introducing a strengths focus to **O**thers (Chapter 6).

2 Identifying and developing strengths in **O**thers (Chapter 7).

3 Supporting **O**thers to manage their weaknesses (Chapter 8).

Introducing a strengths focus to Others

Man's mind, once stretched by a new idea,
never regains its original dimensions.
(Oliver Wendell Holmes Sr, physician and poet)

WE ASSUME YOU MIGHT HAVE READ this far and are feeling enthusiastic about adopting the principles and processes of strengths-focused leadership. The empirical research we referred to (in Chapter 1) provides you with enough of an evidence base to justify the incorporation of a strengths focus into your leadership practice.

But we guess you might be thinking, 'Where do I start? How do I go about introducing the principles of a strengths focus to others? How do I get my team engaged with the strengths idea, rather than feeling like I have imposed the latest management thinking on them?'

In this chapter, we aim to offer you a practical approach for introducing a strengths focus to your team and some suggestions about how you can make a start.

By the end of this chapter you will have answers to the following questions:

1. Why do I want to introduce a strengths focus and what results do I want to see?
2. What can I do to introduce a strengths focus to my team?
3. What would a session introducing a strengths focus look like?
4. How can I continue to incorporate a strengths focus on an ongoing basis?

Why do I want to introduce a strengths focus and what results do I want to see?

Before you start, it is important that you are clear about why you want to introduce a strengths focus and begin with the end in mind.

You may say that you want to find a way of harnessing individuals' natural capacities and allow them to do more of what they do best, which will ultimately drive enhanced performance. You may have other unique reasons for wanting to focus on strengths: maybe there is change happening, maybe there is a need to drive a higher level of engagement and improve staff retention, maybe you want to have a really motivated and high-performing team and see the strengths route as a way to achieve this.

Why not take some time now to think about why you want to introduce a strengths focus to your leadership and what you want to achieve by doing so. Here are some questions to help you:

▍ What outcomes do **I** want to achieve by introducing a strengths focus to my leadership approach?

▍ What outcomes might my **team members** hope for?

▍ Who else has a vested interest in the performance of my team? What might these **stakeholders** hope to see as an outcome?

Are the outcomes for you, your team members and your stakeholders similar? Clearly, the more aligned the joint outcomes are, the easier it will be for you to introduce a strengths focus.

What can I do to introduce a strengths focus to my team?

Where do I start?

It might be that you are already clear about how you want to proceed. For those who are a little less certain, you might see several openings and opportunities and are wondering what to do first.

Before you embark on introducing a strengths focus it is a good idea to provide your team with an initial overview of a strengths focus, what it means, what it involves and why it might be useful.

Start small

You will want to have a plan for enabling your team to harness the benefits of a strengths focus. Our best advice is: don't try to do everything at once. Start small. Pick one area and introduce the strengths approach in small achievable steps that give you and your team some quick wins and build the motivation to continue on the strengths route.

For example, you might introduce strengths to a small sub-team as a pilot, helping them understand the strengths focus, allowing everyone to complete a strengths assessment and have some feedback and discussion around it.

Some leaders decide to introduce a strengths focus in their informal one-to-one discussions. Others introduce the concept of strengths through one of the formal employee processes, such as performance management or appraisal discussions. Some leaders have introduced strengths to a project team who are leading a specific change project and have seen this as a good way to both bond the individuals in the team and ensure that the team performs at its best.

Ten options for introducing a strengths focus

1. Introduce the concept of a strengths focus at a team event and see whether this is something the team would like to explore more (a suggested process for this is offered below).

2. Invite your team members to identify their strengths using one of the many methods outlined (in Chapter 3) and offer them feedback/individual one-to-one coaching.

3. Hold a one-day event where people are introduced to strengths and can find out about their own strengths, having previously completed a strengths assessment.

4. Hold a further one-day event where the team can understand each others' strengths and explore the strengths of the team as a whole.

5. Develop a common vocabulary around strengths – start using the language of strengths.

6. Focus on strengths when agreeing business and development objectives (see Chapters 5 and 13).

7. Include a focus on strengths in recruitment processes (see Chapter 14).

8   Include a focus on strengths in performance management processes such as performance reviews/appraisals (see Chapter 12).

9   Build a team that focuses on strengths (see Chapter 15).

10 Introduce a strengths focus to a team that is managing a specific change (see Chapter 16) or developing strategy (Chapter 17).

What would a session introducing a strengths focus look like?

From our experience, it can be best to offer your team a brief introduction to a strengths focus, giving them an opportunity to understand what a strengths focus is and the benefits it offers, and allowing them a chance to discuss what they like and any concerns they have. This is option 1 in the list above. It also helps to facilitate a couple of brief exercises that are stimulating and allow people to experience the positive impact of talking about strengths.

A session like this usually takes about 2½ hours and can include these areas:

▌ What are strengths?

▌ What is a strengths focus?

▌ Strengths spotting exercise.

▌ How can teams and organisations make the most of strengths?

▌ Discussion.

Drawing on information provided so far, including the empirical evidence for taking a strengths approach, detail about what adopting a strengths focus involves and the practical exercises, we have constructed the content of an 'Introducing a strengths focus' session that you can facilitate for your team. This is shown below. More detailed guidance is available on our website www.sfleadership.co.uk.

Introducing a strengths focus

Timing – no. of minutes	Content
15	**Introduction** Why we are here – context Aims of the session Content of the session

▶

15	**What are strengths?**
	Exercise in pairs:
	'One thing that I am not good at, that I don't enjoy, and that drains me'
	'One thing that I am good at, that I love doing, and that energises me'
	Debrief the exercise: What did you notice?
	Definition of a strength: 'A strength is something that you are good at, that energises and motivates you and gives you great results.'
30	**What is a strengths focus?**
	▌ Why focus on strengths? (Chapter 1)
	▌ Some evidence to support a strengths focus, e.g. Corporate Leadership Council, 2002; Rath and Conchie, 2008 (Chapter 1)
	▌ The benefits of a strengths approach (Chapter 1)
	▌ The business case (Chapter 1)
	▌ What a strengths focus is linked to (Chapter 1)
	▌ Mindset of a strengths focus (Chapter 2)
30	**Strengths-spotting exercise:**
	▌ Introduce the exercise by asking people to 'Write down three occasions when you did something well and really enjoyed doing it.'
	▌ In groups of three, people take turns to talk about their situations whilst others listen and note the strengths they see/hear.
	▌ Each individual hears feedback from their colleagues on the strengths that have been spotted.
	▌ Debrief in the main group – what was useful about that exercise?
30	**How can teams make the most of a strengths approach?**
	Allow people to work in groups to generate their ideas on how a strengths approach can be applied within their team.
	Debrief ideas.
20	**Discussion: A strengths focus – what do we like?**
	Divide into small groups to discuss the following:
	What do we like?
	What are our concerns?
	Hear ideas in the main group.
10	Final questions and next steps.

How can I continue to incorporate a strengths focus on an ongoing basis?

The opportunities for incorporating strengths are many. As you can see from the **MORE** model, the strengths focus can be usefully applied to you as a leader, to those you lead, in your regular day-to-day interactions and in the employee processes that you use.

Let your team guide you

We have found that it is particularly powerful to let teams determine for themselves how they want to apply the strengths approach – after all, it is much more a philosophy and a mindset than it is a set of processes.

For example, your team might want to start by identifying individual strengths and the combined strengths of the team, in order that people can be given the chance to contribute to the team objectives in a way that is aligned with their strengths.

When your team becomes familiar and comfortable with the strengths-focused mindset, and eager to find ways of incorporating a strengths approach, you can go on to look at the processes in the team that can be 'strengthened'. It might be that people in your team have responsibility for some employee processes that affect others in the organisation. If so, a wise approach is to let experts look at their own processes and decide how they might bring a strengths approach into them.

Introducing strengths into a team is something that can be done in a relatively short period of time. As a leader, you do not need to know the whole way forward. Use your team to help you decide which are the next best steps to take on the strengths journey. Here are some practical ideas on the varied approaches you might take.

ACTION POINTS

Introducing a strengths focus to others

1. Be clear about the reasons for introducing a strengths focus to your leadership and to your team. What results are you hoping for?

2. Decide on a method for introducing the concept of strengths to your team.

3 Be clear about what options are available to help your team identify their strengths. For example, will you coach people through completing their 5 Step Strengths Map (see Chapter 3) and R5 Action Plan (see Chapter 4)?

4 Prepare thoroughly for the 'Introducing a strengths focus' session with your team.

5 Think about the different possibilities for starting to introduce strengths to the team's way of working.

6 Allow your team to put forward their own ideas about how a strengths focus can be incorporated into the team's way of working.

7 Agree with the team some first steps for incorporating a strengths focus within the team.

Identifying and developing strengths in Others

Management is about human beings. Its task is to make people capable of joint performance, to make their strengths effective and their weaknesses irrelevant.
(Peter F. Drucker, management consultant, educator and author)

IF YOU NOW HAVE CLARITY about your own strengths and how you can develop them and are feeling a sense of energy and authenticity as a result, you are probably already beginning to ask yourself how you can do the same for others. You may be wondering how you can help those you lead to identify, play to and develop their strengths in order to maximise their own performance and fulfilment at work.

By the end of this chapter you will have answers to the following questions:

1 Why help others identify their strengths?

2 How can I help others identify their strengths?

3 How can I help others develop their strengths?

Why help others identify their strengths?

Many people do not have an active awareness of their strengths. Your team members might know what they are good at, based on their own observations and on feedback, but most of them are unlikely to have consciously differentiated what they are merely good at from those things that really energise and motivate them as well as drive good performance. This is where you can be of help.

When you lead with a strengths focus and help your team members to identify and develop their strengths, these are the benefits you are likely to see in people:

▌ improved performance overall – faster and better results;

▌ more energy for what they want to do;

▌ a wider perspective and a greater awareness of the choices available to them;

▌ enhanced confidence and self-belief, underpinned by a stronger sense of self and who they are;

▌ a higher level of job satisfaction, fulfilment and engagement;

▌ faster personal growth and development.

So, we will now look at how you can achieve these valuable outcomes.

How can I help others identify their strengths?

We have explored the different approaches for identifying your own strengths (in Chapter 3). These same options are available to leaders wanting to move on to helping individuals in their teams identify their strengths. As a reminder, these options fall into three categories that we will look at here:

1 strength spotting;

2 semi-structured assessments, for example using the 5 Step Strengths Map;

3 online assessment.

Whatever approach you choose, in order to maximise the value of the conversation, it is worth thinking about two additional aspects that will enable the conversation to go well and be of most benefit: creating an environment of **trust and rapport**, and **adopting a coaching style**. We will briefly look at what each of these mean.

Trust and rapport

There needs to be a high level of trust and rapport between you and your team member in order for them to feel comfortable discussing their strengths and their weaknesses. Ideally, when you start to talk about strengths they will sense that your intention is positive, especially if you already have a high level of trust and rapport. If that is the case, you will probably find that when you suggest having a conversation to identify their strengths, learned behaviours and weaknesses, you will have a team of individuals eager to have that discussion. Alternatively, you might have some concerns that the level of trust is not yet high enough, and you will therefore need to invest some time in building the rapport and trust. In these situations it can be useful to introduce the strengths- focused approach as part of a team meeting and have a conversation about what people like about the strengths-focused approach and what their reservations are. (For more information about how you can do this, see Chapter 6.)

Adopting a coaching style

It is also essential to adopt a coaching style when helping others identify their strengths. That means asking great questions, listening well and facilitating the process of self-assessment. You may already know that coaching is not about telling someone what you think or what he or she should do. This is particularly relevant with strengths, because only the individual knows what energises them. (See Chapter 11 for more about strengths-focused coaching.)

Notice the difference between these two interactions between a manager and their team member. Both work within the finance function of an organisation providing business support to other functions.

Interaction 1

Manager: So, if we start by looking at your strengths. This might be something that you haven't thought too much about before. Tell me, what sort of things are you good at doing and really love doing at work? In other words, what sort of things really energise you and give you great results too?

Individual: Hmm. Good question. Well, my first response might have been to say that my strengths were in analysing information and producing accurate information. I think I'm good at that, but I don't find it all that energising. It's just my job. What I do find energising is going out and talking with people in the other functions, and I know I'm good at that. Now I think about it, that is probably a real strength of mine.

Manager: Yes, I've noticed how much you enjoy that too. And, you get some great results there as well. What else do you really enjoy and find you get good results in?

Interaction 2

Manager: So, if we start by looking at your strengths. This might be something that you haven't thought too much about before. Tell me, what sort of things are you good at doing and really love doing at work? In other words, what sort of things really energise you and give you great results, too? For example, if I can just help you out here, I think you have real strengths in analysing information and achieving a high level of accuracy. I've noticed how people really appreciate that. And you seem to enjoy sharing that accurate information. What do you think?

Individual: Yes, well, I suppose you are right.

Manager: And what other strengths do you think you have. Around people, for example?

Individual: Yes, I like talking with people in the business functions and I am good at that.

No doubt you can spot the difference between these two examples of interactions, and you probably sense the de-energising impact on the individual when they are told what to think.

As demonstrated in the examples, there may be scope for offering some feedback about your own observations, but it is only the individual him- or herself who can really say what it is that they enjoy and what energises them. Remember, it is easy to fall into the trap of mistaking something that someone is good at for a strength – if it doesn't energise and motivate them, it isn't a strength!

So, we will now look at the three different ways of helping people identify their strengths.

1. **Strength spotting:** Identifying strengths is not a one-off process. Strengths-focused leaders help other people to articulate for themselves what they believe their strengths to be, and they also always have their antennae out ready to notice strengths in others and bring them to their attention. For example, a manager might say to a team member at the end of a conversation: 'This is really good work you are doing, and I've noticed how much you have enjoyed the challenge of solving the problem and getting to a result. I think that's a real strength of yours. What do you think?'

   By spotting others' strengths and pointing them out, you will be helping others become more aware of their strengths, and then they will be able to use and apply them more.

Remember that you will be able to notice someone using strengths any time that they are performing well and appear to be:

▌ highly motivated;

▌ demonstrating a higher level of energy than they usually do;

▌ really enjoying themselves;

▌ getting a 'buzz' from what they are doing;

▌ learning quickly;

▌ showing emotions to a higher degree than they usually do, such as enthusiasm, happiness, humour;

▌ demonstrating more confidence;

▌ getting things done quickly.

However, not everyone demonstrates their inner energies and emotions in an external way. If you are familiar with psychometrics, you may know how people who are more naturally introverted tend to experience their emotions internally and prefer not to externalise them to everyone. So, it is always best to exercise some caution when strengths spotting and remember that each individual is their own best judge of whether something is energising to them. Starting a dialogue about possible strengths that you have observed is a great way of helping individuals share their own experience of an activity and assess whether the activity has revealed their strengths or not.

2 **Semi-structured assessments:** We believe that the 5 Step Strengths Map (described in detail in Chapter 3) is one of the most practical methods for helping someone to identify their strengths. The 5 Step Strengths Map approach is useful in that it also identifies untapped strengths, weaknesses and their learned behaviours (those things that people are good at but that drain them).

The 5 Step Strengths Map framework of questions offered to you (in Chapter 3) to help you identify your own strengths is the same that we would suggest you use to help your team members identify their strengths. Here is the 5 Step Strengths Map and associated questions again for you to use with your team members. This can be downloaded as a template from our website at www.sfleadership. co.uk. You might want to go back (Chapter 3) and have another look at the example we gave you of a conversation with Mary as she was taken through the process.

Exercise: Your 5 Step Strengths Map

Use the map to capture your team members' responses to the questions and help them 'map' their strengths. They should be able to identify up to six or seven main strengths, and a similar number of untapped strengths. It is usual to identify no more than three or four weaknesses. If they find more, they are trying too hard!

Steps 1–3: The activities that energise you

1. Your strengths	**2. Your untapped strengths**	**3. Your overplayed strengths**
• What do you love doing in your work? *(Think back to situations you have been most energised at work)* • What behaviours and attributes do you enjoy using, demonstrate well and use regularly? • When do you use these strengths? What examples can you think of? • What do you enjoy about using them? How do they make you feel?	• What do you love doing but just don't get the opportunity to do very often? Perhaps strengths you used in previous jobs or roles? • When do you currently use this strength/these strengths? • What do you enjoy about using it? How does it make you feel? • On a scale of 0–10, where 0 is not all and 10 is ideal, how much do you currently use that strength?	• Where might you be using some of your strengths too much? • What's the impact? • Where might it be the wrong kind of situation to use them?

Steps 4–5: The activities that drain your energy

4. Your learned behaviours	**5. Your weaknesses**
• What things are you good at, but don't enjoy or that drain you to do them? • What sort of things do you struggle to get started with?	• What do you perform less well in and also find to be a drain on your energy? • How does this weakness currently impact your role and work? • How important is it to your success in the role?

3 **Online assessment:** Previously (in Chapter 3) we detailed the benefits of using an online strengths assessment tool to identify strengths and weaknesses and we provided you with an overview of four of the comprehensive tools currently available: Strengthsfinder™, Strengthscope™, Realise2© and VIA (Values in Action). If you have read this far and have completed your own online strengths assessment, it is likely that you have opted for one of these for good reasons and will possibly choose the same tool for your team.

You may well have narrowed down your choice of assessment based on whether you can conduct the process yourself without the need for a third party (Strengthsfinder™, VIA and Realise2©), whether it includes 360 degree feedback, and whether it is possible to generate a team strengths profile, which clearly has additional benefits beyond team members merely knowing their strengths as individuals. (Realise2©, Strengthscope™ and VIA (Pro Version) offer this option, but only accredited practitioners can conduct this.)

With a finite budget for team development a question that you might ask yourself is, 'How can I do this in the most economical way?' Depending on your budget and what you need to achieve, you have a number of options available to you:

▌ online assessment and line manager debrief;

▌ online assessment with one-to-one debrief by an external coach/ facilitator;

▌ online assessment with group debrief by an external facilitator;

▌ online assessment, one-to-one coaching debrief, plus an additional day to explore individual strengths and team strengths.

 Please go to our website www.sfleadership.co.uk for some case study examples of the above options.

How can I help others develop their strengths?

We have introduced several different approaches that you can take to develop your own strengths (in Chapter 4). If you have taken part in some of the suggested activities, you are no doubt ready to give some of the approaches a go with your own team and we now offer you some further guidelines for doing this. Remember, to get the full benefit from the strengths approach, people need not just to know their strengths; they need to use them and develop them too. And also remember that developing a strength may not be about using it more – just using a strength in increasing quantities can lead to it being a strength overplayed if it is not applied in the right way and in the right context.

Selecting the 'right' strengths to develop

When your team members have identified their strengths, perhaps using the 5 Step Strengths Map, you can go on to help them select the 'right' strengths to develop.

We would suggest that any individual selects only three to five strengths to develop. You might find that people have many more possible strengths to develop, so to help identify the most relevant ones to focus on, you can ask them these questions:

▌ Are you good at this compared to others or compared to what is expected of you in your role?

▌ Do others agree that this is a strength?

▌ How do you feel when you think about using this strength more? (Ideally energised, enthusiastic and motivated)

▌ To what degree does your role require you to use this strength more?

▌ To what degree does this team require you to use this strength more?

▌ To what degree does this organisation require you to use this strength more?

Five ways of developing strengths

Having helped people in your team to identify strengths they want to develop, the next stage is to support them in choosing some ways to develop these strengths, including identifying specific actions to take. Using the R5 Action Plan (see Chapter 4) to structure this conversation about developing strengths might be all you need to do to ensure your team member has a range of ideas to get to work on.

Here are some further options for developing team members' strengths:

1. **Testing the limits of a strength by pushing for higher levels of competency.** This is about helping others to extend the limits of their strengths to see whether by doing so they can achieve higher levels of performance, engagement, motivation, etc.

2. **Asking others for feedback, ideas and suggestions.** This is about individuals checking in with colleagues and stakeholders as to whether a strength is being optimised and whether there are other ways the strength can be applied for mutual benefit. As well as

getting feedback, you can use the concept of Feedforward,[1] which involves the individual getting suggestions from others about what they would like to see the person do to apply their strengths more.

3 **Learning new skills or taking on new tasks.** This involves exploring new territories that will provide opportunities to apply and, therefore, develop the strength.

4 **Coaching or training others.** A very effective way of building on and developing a strength is to help others to develop a strength in the same area.

5 **Incorporating strengths development into learning and development objectives.** An individual's development plan, as part of the annual performance review or appraisal process, provides a great opportunity for planning to develop strengths.

6 **Finding a coach or mentor.** This is a good opportunity for you to offer some coaching support to your team member. Alternatively, they might benefit from someone else in the organisation mentoring them and they could think about the value of selecting a mentor who possesses the strengths that they want to develop, although this is not essential for an effective mentoring relationship.

All the above options for developing strengths mirror the various options offered to you as the leader for developing your own strengths. You can therefore refer back (to Chapter 3) for more detail on all the above options, along with some examples of what this can look like in practice.

To support you in applying these different approaches with your team members, here is a comprehensive set of coaching questions that you can use.

Testing the limits of a strength by pushing for higher levels of competency

▌ How could you use this strength more?

▌ How could you apply this strength to achieve an even higher level of performance?

---

[1] Goldsmith, M. *FeedForward*. www.marshallgoldsmithfeedforward.com Accessed 21.7.14.

How could you apply this strength to achieve an even higher level of job satisfaction and fulfilment?

How can you do more of what is already working? (What are the risks of this? e.g. overplaying a strength)

What other ways can you apply this strength? What difference will that make? What will be good about that for you/others/the team/the organisation? Could there be a negative impact?

In what other contexts/situations could you apply this strength? What difference will that make? What will be good about that for you/others/the team/the organisation?

Asking others for feedback, ideas and suggestions

What do you know about how others perceive this strength and whether you apply it in the right amount in the right context?

How could you find out? Who could you ask?

What do you know about whether others would like to see more of or less of this strength?

What do you think others might suggest to you for developing this strength?

Who can you go to, to ask for feedback, ideas and suggestions?

What specific strengths would you like to get feedback from others on? Who could you ask?

What strengths would you like to get specific Feedforward suggestions from others on? Who could you go to?

Learning new skills or taking on new tasks

What new or different tasks could you take on that will give you the opportunity to play to this strength?

What is it about that task that will allow you to use your strength?

What will the impact of that be on you/your role/the team/the organisation?

What new skills have you always wanted to learn?

What is the link between this and the strength you want to develop?

What can you do to learn this skill?

How can I help/support you?

What could you do outside of work that would allow you to play to and develop this strength?

What do you need to do to make that happen?

Coaching or training others

Who might benefit from your support in helping them develop in this area for themselves?

What could you do to see whether this is something the person would like to do?

Who might benefit from your coaching in this area?

What opportunities are there for you to share this strength with the other members of the team, in order that they might learn from you?

Incorporating strengths development into learning and development objectives

What ideas for development have arisen from your discussions so far about your performance and goals?

What are some of the key strengths that you would like to build upon as part of your development plan?

What behaviours or strengths are in need of development and improvement?

What development requirements have been discussed as being necessary to support the achievement of your objectives for the next period (skill, knowledge, behaviour or strengths)?

What development requirements have been discussed in order for you to achieve your career aspirations?

Finding a coach or mentor

What coaching support would you value from me as your manager?

If I were to offer you some coaching support, what would you like to focus on in these conversations?

What value might you find in having a mentor from within the organisation? Is this something you would like to do?

How would you like a mentor to support you in developing your strengths?

What sort of strengths would you value in a mentor?

Here's an example of some of these questions being used in a developmental conversation. Michelle, a Buyer in a retail organisation, was helping Carl, a Buying Assistant, to develop his strengths and to plan to use them more. Michelle is exploring option 1, testing the limits of the strength. This is how the conversation went:

Michelle: Carl, you say you have a strength of being able to relate to people. (Relationship Builder) I agree that you do this with real empathy and compassion. I have noticed it and your team members have, too. It's something that we all appreciate. How do you think you could you use this strength more?

Carl: Well, that's good to hear. I've been thinking about how I could use this strength more and it's definitely a strength that I could use more with supplier interactions. I think I could take a more active role in discussions with suppliers and help to build positive relationships.

Michelle: How do you think you could do this?

Carl: I think if I were to draw on my strength of empathy, particularly when dealing with conflict situations, then I could help get a better outcome from discussions.

Michelle: That sounds great. How do you think you could apply these strengths to achieve an even higher level of job satisfaction and fulfilment for yourself?

Carl: Well, by using my strengths in these situations, seeing it as an opportunity to build relationships and use my strengths, I think I will feel less intimidated by potential conflict situations.

Michelle: Sounds good. What other ways can you apply these strengths?

Carl: I think I could also use these strengths to build stronger relationships with the Senior Management Team.

Michelle: What difference will that make?

Carl: Well, they'll certainly get to know me more. I'll also feel that maybe I have more of a voice if I can get to talk to them more often.

Michelle: What will be good about that for you/others/the team/the organisation?

Carl: It will definitely be good for me to raise my profile and get known, but it's always good for being productive at work if there are strong working relationships. It might help with my career progression, too.

Michelle: In what other contexts/situations could you apply this strength?

Carl: Hmm . . . Good question. I'll have a think about that and let you know.

Identifying and developing strengths in Others

1 Ensure that your team are open to exploring their strengths.

2 Ensure that there is a high level of trust and rapport between you and your team members. If not, think about what you need to do to build this trust.

3 Revisit what you know about a coaching approach – you will need to draw on these skills to explore people's strengths with them.

4 Decide on the approach you want to take to help your team members identify their strengths, using one of the methods described (in Chapter 3).

5 Set aside time to have conversations with each of your team members about how they can develop their strengths. Start by using the R5 Action Plan (see Chapter 4) and, if needed, explore some of the other options for developing strengths.

6 Remember to always take a coaching approach!

8 Supporting Others to manage their weaknesses

Everybody is a genius. But if you judge a fish by its ability to climb a tree, it will live its whole life believing that it is stupid.
(Albert Einstein, theoretical physicist)

By now you will realise that strengths-focused leadership does not mean ignoring weaknesses. If a weakness is critical to an individual's ability to perform well, it needs to be addressed as a priority alongside developing strengths.

If you have read this far, we expect you have also developed a more balanced view of your weaknesses and have decided upon a few strategies to respond to and manage those weaknesses where they are important or significant enough. And we suspect you are now ready to think about how you can support others to do the same.

By the end of this chapter you will have answers to the following questions:

1 Why help others identify and manage their weaknesses?

2 How can I help others identify their weaknesses?

3 How can I help others manage their weaknesses?

Why help others identify and manage their weaknesses?

It is important to remember that your team member only has a weakness if there is something that they do not do well *and* it is critically important to their and the team's performance. If it isn't important, our advice is to leave well alone and focus on the strengths that will make the biggest difference to performance.

There are only a few reasons why, as a leader who focuses on strengths, you would want to focus on weaknesses. The few reasons we can think of are:

▌ you or your team members have identified a weakness that is critical to their performance and it could be a potential derailer for them;

▌ your team member's weakness stands out to others and is impacting others' performance;

▌ your team member has an inherent desire to focus on their weaknesses to improve their performance – it may take a little more time for them to accept a strengths focus and you need to go at their pace;

▌ your team member is in the wrong job – this may provide a great opportunity to find them a role that is more suited to their strengths;

▌ you want to encourage the team to do complementary role sharing. To do this they may tell one another about their weaknesses as well as their strengths. By sharing weaknesses they can look at how one person's weakness can be supported by another person's strength.

How can I help others identify their weaknesses?

If your team member is self-aware and alert to their significant weaknesses, then you are in an easier position and you can begin to support them straight away by adopting some of the strengths-focused approaches we are going to offer you in this chapter. However, it may be that your team member is not aware of the existence of a significant weakness and is blind to the negative impact that it is having on both their own and others' performance. In this case, you will need to select an appropriate strategy for bringing this significant weakness to your team member's attention and gain their agreement to do something about it.

Here are six approaches that a strengths-focused leader can use to help their team member identify or acknowledge any significant weaknesses and ensure that they are motivated to take some action to address the weakness:

1 Talk about strengths first.

2 Use the 5 Step Strengths Map (see Chapter 3).

3 Explore the impact of strengths overplayed.

4 Offer feedback.

5 Introduce 360 degree feedback within the team.

6 Encourage the person to do an online assessment of strengths, ideally with 360 degree feedback built in.

Talk about strengths first

When broaching the subject of your team member's weaknesses, it is always a good idea to start the conversation on a more energising note by exploring with them their strengths. This will ensure that they are in a much more positive, energised and open-minded state when it comes to identifying any weaknesses. In fact, most high-performing team members will tend to be eager to explore and eliminate any significant weaknesses, but it's always best to encourage people to explore their strengths first.

Use the 5 Step Strengths Map

The 5 Step Strengths Map offers a logical structure for helping people identify their strengths and their weaknesses (see Chapter 3). In addition, it helps people identify strengths that are being underutilised, learned behaviours (things that people have learned to be good at, but are not energising strengths) and also, strengths that are being overplayed. Using this framework with your team member will help them build their awareness of their strengths and weaknesses and the impact they are having, and it also offers you the opportunity to add your feedback based on your own observations.

Explore the impact of strengths overplayed

Any strength that is used too much or used in the wrong context can easily become a weakness. For example, a strength of being able to take charge of situations and exercise leadership, if overplayed, might lead to an individual coming across as too autocratic and overly directive. You can help your team member describe what their strengths overplayed might look like and explore whether they are demonstrating any of the characteristics being described. It is usually easier to accept something being a weakness if it is perceived as a strength that is being overplayed and needs to be regulated.

Offer feedback

If you have applied the three suggestions above, you may find that your team member is now aware of any significant weaknesses and is ready to create a plan for managing them. However, there may also be a need for you to offer your own feedback. A useful approach to delivering feedback is to describe the behaviour that you have seen and the impact that it has on you, and, if appropriate to share, on others. Sometimes it feels right to share your feedback directly, and at other times it can be helpful to use more of a coaching approach and encourage your direct report to self-evaluate. Once again, it's always good to start with the positives first, identifying some good things that you can offer feedback on.

Here's an example to show you how a feedback conversation might go in practice. This is an excerpt from a conversation where the leader, Tim, the Financial Controller, is debriefing Carol's 360 degree report. Carol is a Finance Business Partner and her role involves offering expertise and support to help colleagues in other departments make better business decisions.

Tim: *So, we've had a look at the highest ratings on your 360 degree feedback and identified some very clear strengths. How about the lower ratings. What do you notice about those?*

Carol: *Well, I can see from the ratings and also from the comments that there seems to be a need for me to be much more collaborative in my dealings with other departments.*

Tim: *Which specific departments do you believe this refers to?*

Carol: *I think it is the marketing team. They just don't get the need to stick to budgets and to think about these things before making decisions. What's the point of collaborating, if they go off and do what they want anyway?*

Tim: *How important is collaboration to your role as Finance Business Partner?*

Carol: *Well, of course it's important. Yes – very. But I do go and talk to them quite a lot. I always seem to be in meetings.*

Tim: *What do you think has led to you getting lower ratings for your collaborative approach?*

Carol: *Well, I guess that it's because I tend to appear a bit negative in my dealings with them. They think I'm all doom and gloom.*

Tim: *What impact do you think this has?*

Carol: *Well, they probably don't enjoy working with me, and I can tell that they try to avoid me if they can so that they can sidestep me and do things their way.*

Tim: *And what is the impact of that?*

Carol: *Well, it means that I'm not doing the advisory part of my role very well.*

Tim: *I'd agree with that. I have noticed that there are times when you have appeared to be quite argumentative and this can really damage the relationships you have. As a business partner, it is important to be able to have a good rapport with people before you can even begin to collaborate and, subsequently, influence them. I can see your other strengths are coming into play here, such as your Detail Focus and Strategic Thinking, and this is at the expense of the all-important Collaboration. In my view, this is something quite significant for you to address first in your development plan. What do you think?*

Introduce 360 degree feedback within the team

360 degree feedback, whereby colleagues offer anonymous feedback and ratings on each other's performance in certain behaviours, competencies or even strengths, is a very useful means of giving your team members the opportunity to see themselves through others' eyes. Where 360 degree feedback includes the opportunity for colleagues to add comments as well as numeric rating, this can be especially helpful in enabling people to identify both their strengths and any significant weaknesses.

By debriefing the 360 degree feedback with your team member, and ensuring that you stay focused on strengths and what is working as well as what is not working, you will be able to help them also identify any weaknesses. Remember that it is important to discuss the relevance of any weaker areas. Only if it is critical for the individual's performance should it be selected as a significant weakness for them to address.

Encourage the person to do an online assessment of strengths, ideally with 360 degree feedback built in

One last option is to consider asking your team to identify their strengths and relative weaknesses using one of the online strengths identification tools (outlined in Chapter 3) that also has a 360 degree feedback element within it. This could be a great way of introducing a strengths focus to your whole team and an opportunity to enhance team performance by raising awareness of individual strengths and alerting team members to their potential weaknesses. When all the team members' strengths and weaknesses are shared, this provides an opportunity to explore complementary role sharing, where team members can work out the best way to share tasks in ways that maximise the application of strengths and minimise the need to use weaknesses.

How can I help others manage their weaknesses?

We have offered you several ways for managing your own weaknesses, all of which are approaches that you can use to help others in managing theirs (see Chapter 4). If your team member identifies a weakness, you can help them understand whether it is important to address the weakness and whether by not doing so their performance will continue to be adversely affected.

Here are nine approaches that you can use to help your team members manage their weaknesses:

1. Create a picture of success.
2. Offer Feedforward suggestions.
3. Regulate a strength overplayed.
4. Help your team member find a role model.
5. Help your team member to identify and plan to use some alternative behaviours.
6. Help your team member to find other strengths to help manage the weakness.
7. Consider complementary role sharing in a team context.
8. Build managing the weakness into a development plan.
9. Consider a different role.

Create a picture of success

Help your team member to be clear about what successfully turning around the weakness will look like. What will they be doing when they have eradicated this weakness, and what will the positive impact of that be?

Offer Feedforward suggestions

Your team member might welcome some suggestions from you about what they could do to improve in their area of weakness. It will be even more powerful if your team member decides to solicit Feedforward suggestions from some colleagues and stakeholders of their choice. You can help them determine what they would like to get suggestions on and from whom. (See Chapter 4 for the process of using Feedforward.)

Regulate a strength overplayed

Some weaknesses are the result of strengths being overplayed. When your team member looks at their weakness in this light, is it often much easier for them to identify ways to regulate or 'tone down' the application of this strength such that it is no longer a weakness.

Help your team member find a role model

If your team member wants to master a new behaviour they can find someone who demonstrates the behaviour well and carefully observe what they do, in order that they can aim to use similar behaviours. You can help your team member identify a role model and what aspects of the individual they have in mind they want to copy or model.

Help your team member to identify and plan to use some alternative behaviours

If you have done a good job of helping your team member describe what success looks like, then they should very easily describe some new behaviours that they want to apply in order to respond to the weakness. You can coach them to identify several opportunities to apply a new behaviour.

The more specific you can get people to be, the better, and here are some coaching questions that can help you do this:

▌ Imagine this weakness has gone away, what will you be doing?

▌ What will you be saying?

▌ How will you be feeling?

▌ What will you be seeing?

▌ What results will you be getting that you are not getting now?

▌ What will be good about that?

▌ Thinking about what you will be doing, what are the specific behaviours that people will see you using?

▌ When are you already using these behaviours? How have you been able to do that? What has been the impact?

▌ What opportunities have you got to apply or use these behaviours more?

▌ When else?

▌ What are you going to do now?

▌ When are you going to start?

▌ What is going to be good about that for you, others and the organisation?

Help your team member find other strengths to help manage the weakness

You might find that however good you are in helping your team member design a plan for applying new behaviours, there is still a lingering sense of inertia. This should not surprise you – after all, the thought of using our weakness is going to feel very de-energising. You can address this inertia by helping your team member find ways of drawing on their strengths in order to help them manage their weaknesses. It's very interesting to see how the energy shifts and suddenly the idea of addressing the 'weakness' becomes much more appealing.

To give you an example, Tina wanted to become more confident around very senior managers and to be more assertive and confident when discussing differences of opinion. She knew that her slight sense of intimidation around senior management was something that had been with her for some time, and was also something she wanted to get over. I (Kathy) explored her strengths and Tina discovered that she had several strengths that she could bring to bear when in dialogue with senior management. She specifically saw that such interactions gave her an opportunity to use her strength of building rapport and connecting with people. She also had a strength in problem solving and loved doing puzzles, so she decided to view the subject matter of any of the more tricky conversations with senior managers as an opportunity to solve a problem together, which made the thought of these conversations much more appealing.

Consider complementary role sharing in a team context

It can be very draining if we regularly have to exercise behaviours that are weaknesses for us. If the behaviour in question is critical to the person's role, another way of helping them managing their weakness might be to find a colleague or colleagues who have the behaviour as a strength. A team can be involved in looking at one another's relative strengths and weaknesses and use this greater knowledge of one another to share roles and tasks according to strengths. Then tasks that require a strength that you do not have can be taken on by someone who does have it.

Build managing the weakness into a development plan

Finally, there is always the option of creating a development objective to address the weakness. However, we would recommend that you only add such objectives if the weakness seriously needs to be addressed and is a potential 'derailer' for the individual. Objectives to address significant weaknesses also need to be balanced with objectives to develop strengths. Imagine how de-energising a development plan might be if it only contains plans to respond to weaknesses. When making sure that any development objective has a plan to achieve it, you can draw on the different suggestions above to help the individual select some actions that they find motivational and energising to them. (See Chapter 13 for ideas on how to have a strengths-focused development discussion.)

Consider a different role

Sometimes the discussion about strengths and weaknesses leads to the realisation that your team member is in the wrong role. If the role cannot be adjusted to allow your team member to play to their strengths, this provides a great opening to have discussions about roles that would be more suited to their strengths and much better for them in the long term.

ACTION POINTS

Supporting **O**thers to manage their weaknesses

1 Take some time to consider each of your team members. In your view, what are their strengths and do they have any significant weaknesses? What is the impact of these significant weaknesses?

▶

2   Consider how aware each team member is of any significant weaknesses. Depending on their current level of awareness, decide on the most appropriate way to discuss these weaknesses and create a plan to address them.

3   Work with each team member to create a plan to address any significant weaknesses.

4   Check in regularly with your direct report and offer feedback on progress and changes that you have observed.

Regular conversations

Silence is one of the great arts of conversation.
(Marcus Tullius Cicero, Roman philosopher, politician and lawyer)

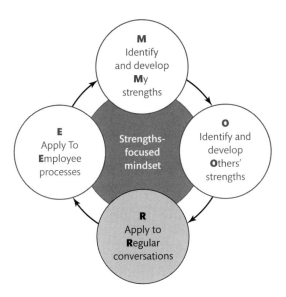

The 'R' of the **MORE** model stands for 'Regular conversations'.

For you to know that you have really embedded a strengths-focused mindset into your everyday behaviour, we believe that it will be useful to consider how it will show itself in your regular conversations with your team and other stakeholders back at work. We address the typical workplace settings for those conversations in our next three chapters:

1 Applying a strengths focus to day-to-day conversations (Chapter 9).

2 Strengths-focused meetings (Chapter 10).

3 Strengths-focused coaching (Chapter 11).

These conversations are the places where you will model the way. You may tell your team that you are adopting a strengths-focused approach to leadership. They will judge the reality of that in what they experience in interactions and conversation with you. These day-to-day interactions are a hugely valuable opportunity for you to influence performance and engagement. Recent research[1] suggests that day-to-day conversations make more impact that any organisational performance management process. We will now explain how it is done.

---

[1] Oberoi, M. and Rajgarhia, P (2013) 'What Your Performance Management System Needs Most', *Gallup Business Journal*. Accessed 13.02.14 from http://businessjournal.gallup.com/content/161546/performance-management-system-needs.aspx.

Applying a strengths focus to day-to-day conversations

The meeting of two personalities is like the contact of two chemical substances: if there is any reaction, both are transformed.
(Carl Jung, psychologist)

SO, AT THIS POINT, you will have understood how to help team members play to their strengths, and now it's about keeping this focus on strengths alive, so that it continues to make a difference to performance.

You may be wondering:

How do I remember all this?

How do I keep it alive day-to-day?

How do I build it in to 'business as usual'?

These are excellent questions and one way of answering all of them is to build up daily strengths-focused habits or behaviours. This chapter will show you how to do it.

By the end of this chapter you will have answers to the following questions:

1 How do I build a strengths-focused mindset and apply the day-to-day behaviours that come from it and reinforce it?

2 What's the difference between a strengths-focused and a weakness-focused conversation?

3 How do I conduct one-to-one conversations with team members that will build confidence, motivation and strength and increase performance?

How do I build a strengths-focused mindset and apply the day-to-day behaviours that come from it and reinforce it?

Previously (in Chapter 2) we presented the link between mindset and behaviour. Essentially the idea is that your mindset, or way of thinking, drives your behaviours. We also clarified the ways of thinking that characterise strengths-focused leadership.

The mindset of a strengths-focused leader

Me

▌ I am the best leader I can be when I am being authentic and playing to my own strengths.

▌ As a great leader I don't need to be strong at everything, and others can bring the strengths that I may not have.

Others

▌ Everyone has strengths that can be harnessed and built on.

Performance

▌ People perform at their best when expectations are clear and aligned as closely as possible with their strengths.

▌ People will perform better, be more motivated and engaged, and make a stronger contribution if they are enabled to play to their strengths.

▌ Our strengths are most effective when we use them at the right time, in the right situation, and the right amount. Strengths can be overused and underused.

Developing people

▌ Helping people identify their strengths helps them use them more.

▌ People develop faster when I focus on building on their strengths.

Teamwork

▌ Teams can play to their strengths more if they identify one another's strengths.

▌ Aligning the individual strengths in the team to the tasks and goals of the team will increase our success.

Weakness

▎ Celebrating strengths and what is working gives people the energy to address their weaknesses and what is working less well or not working at all.

▎ I view my own and others' weaknesses from a position of strength – looking at how we can use our strengths to address any significant weaknesses

We have given you the opportunity to fully assimilate these ideas, since they permeate every aspect of this book's content. There are twelve of them though, under six headings, and perhaps that's a lot to remember. So to simplify them, and to show you how to put them into practice in your everyday work, we present the following three straightforward principles that you can regularly use and assess yourself against that will embed this mindset:

1 Start with an outcome focus.

2 Focus on what's working.

3 Manage weakness from strength.

Exercise: Assessing my day-to-day behaviours

You may now want to assess how well you follow these three principles.

1 = totally disagree and 5 = totally agree.

My day-to-day behaviours	1	2	3	4	5
1. Start with an outcome focus: I am always clear with people (including myself) on what needs to be achieved and what is expected of the team and individuals in order to achieve it, and I believe we have the strengths to achieve our goals.					
2. Focus on what's working: Every day I focus on what works and what people are doing well, in order to identify and develop strengths, and achieve our goals.					
3. Manage weakness from strength: By always focusing on what works and what people are doing well, I help them find the energy to make things work even better, and to manage their weaknesses from strength.					

> Assessing yourself in this way will suggest the areas you want to pay particular attention to in the rest of this chapter. Using the conversational tools that follow will help you to make a habit of thinking in these ways, increasing your ability to create a strengths-focused culture and a high-performing team.

These three principles come out of, and embed, a strengths-focused mindset. We will clarify what we mean by them before we go on to look at how they translate into our everyday conversations and interactions.

Principle 1

Start with an outcome focus. *I am always clear with people on what needs to be achieved and what is expected of the team and individuals in order to achieve it, and I believe we have the strengths to achieve our goals.*

Countless books on the psychology of success point to the wisdom of knowing very clearly the outcome you want to achieve. 'Begin with the end in mind', said Stephen Covey, the bestselling author of *The 7 Habits of Highly Effective People.*[1] The idea crops up everywhere. The Gallup Q12[2] is a 12-item questionnaire used by many large organisations around the world to measure employee engagement. Employees complete a set of 12 questions. These are listed in order of priority. So Question 1 clarifies the place to start in building engagement. It says: 'I know what is expected of me at work.'

We very much agree with this idea. If you want to help people use their strengths effectively, it will be important for them to know what outcomes they need to achieve and, therefore, what to focus their strengths on.

Principle 2

Focus on what's working. *Every day I focus on what works and what people are doing well, in order to identify and develop strengths, and achieve our goals.*

---

[1]   Covey, S. R. (2004) *The 7 Habits of Highly Effective People*, New York, Simon & Schuster.

[2]   Wagner, R. and Harter, J. K. (2006) *12: The Elements of Great Managing*, New York, Gallup Press.

The fields of Solution Focus[3] and Appreciative Enquiry[4] have proved the value of focusing on what's working, rather than on what's not working. One writer captured it succinctly – '*Problem talk creates problems – solution talk creates solutions.*'[5]

We've already identified evidence on how people's performance improves more when their manager focuses appraisal discussions on building strengths. Other recent research found that a group of leaders receiving 360 degree feedback were three times more successful in their (perceived) development when they focused on building their strengths rather than fixing their weaknesses.[6]

A manager with a focus on what's working will be starting their weekly team meeting by asking people to share their recent successes. Starting this way creates a resourceful energy in the group. In addition, the stories of the successes can be explored so that the team can identify the ingredients and principles of creating more successes.

Principle 3

Manage weakness from strength. *By always focusing on what works and what people are doing well, I help them find the energy to make things work even better, and to manage their weaknesses from strength.*

It may not be the way that many organisations and managers approach it, but, when you think about it, it makes sense. If you want to fix what's not working, or to improve things, or to deal with your weaknesses, it's going to be much easier for you to do that from a position of strength. 'How can you bring your strengths to bear on this?' we often ask the people we coach.

T. H. White, former president of GTE Telephone Operations, put it this way: 'If we dissect what we do right and apply the lessons to what we do wrong, we can solve our problems and energize the organisation at the same time. . . . We cannot ignore problems, but we just need to approach them from the other side.'

---

[3] Jackson, P. and McKergow, M. (2002) *The Solutions Focus: The SIMPLE way to positive change*, Clerkenwell, Nicholas Brealey Publishing.

[4] Cooperrider, D. L. and Srivastva, S. (1987) 'Appreciative Inquiry in Organizational Life', *Research in Organizational Change and Development* 1, pp. 129–69.

[5]   De Shazer, S. Quoted in Berg, I. K. and P. Szabo, P. (2005). *Brief Coaching for Lasting Solutions*, London, W.W. Norton & Co., Inc.

[6]   Zenger, J. H., et al. (2012). *How to Be Exceptional: Drive leadership success by magnifying your strengths*, New York, McGraw-Hill.

What's the difference between a strengths-focused and a weakness-focused conversation?

It's important for you to know what these principles look like in real conversations. The following example gives you a flavour of conversations that are strength- and solution-focused, and compares them to those that are more weakness- and problem-focused. In the strengths-focused versions, the leader's interactions have a 'coaching' style, one that empowers the person(s) to come up with their own answers, rather than have the leader tell them what to do. We realise that both approaches (tell and ask) can be appropriate, depending on the situation. In our experience it is the coaching style that leaders are less able to call on when they need it, and so they often find themselves taking a 'tell' approach even when it is not the best style for the situation. We will explore this point in more depth later (in Chapter 11 on strengths-focused coaching).

You'll find strengths in your team members if, in your conversations with them, you look for what things are going well, how these are being achieved, and what positive impact they are having. As well as this type of conversation being able to unearth strengths, it will also build further confidence and motivation, two key elements in high performance.

Here is what this looks like in practice.

Principle 1

Start with an outcome focus. *I am always clear with people (including myself) on what needs to be achieved and what is expected of the team and individuals in order to achieve it, and I believe we have the strengths to achieve our goals.*

My interactions with individuals in one-to-one situations

Weakness focus and problem focus	Strengths focus and solution focus
At the beginning of every day/week/ project:	At the beginning of every day/week/ project:
Manager: So Emma, this is an important project. Don't let us down on this one, please. **Emma:** What do you mean?	**Manager:** So Emma, how clear are you about the outcome we need with the Delta project? **Emma:** Yeah, pretty clear thanks.

Manager: I'll get such a lot of grief up the line if we don't deliver on this one. They're already giving me a hard time, let's not give them any more ammunition? **Emma:** So how long have I got? **Manager:** Not long. Just get it to me as soon as you can? **Emma:** And is there a spec on the deliverables? **Manager:** You're joking, aren't you? I'm the last to know anything round here. Just give them enough to avoid any complaints. **Emma:** Charming . . . **Manager:** Well it's not exactly fun for me either you know. Just get it done Emma, will you. **Emma:** Hmmmm . . .	**Manager:** Great. And how confident do you feel about delivering it to the quality spec and in this time frame? **Emma:** Well, fairly confident about most of it. It's just the number crunching on the budget that I'm not so confident about. **Manager:** OK, Emma. What would support you best with this? **Emma:** Well, Ash is brilliant on the numbers. If I could get him to check mine at the end of each week I'd feel much more confident. **Manager:** Great. I'm sure Ash will be up for that. There might need to be a latte or two involved though, eh? Emma, I'm sure you'll do a great job. We'll talk same time next week, OK? **Emma:** Yeah, sure. Thanks.

Principle 2

Focus on what's working. *Every day I focus on what works and what people are doing well in order to identify and develop strengths, and achieve our goals.*

My interactions with individuals in one-to-one situations

Weakness focus and problem focus	Strengths focus and solution focus
On a specific project:	On a specific project:
Manager: So, Emma, have you not got that project finished yet? **Emma:** What?! **Manager:** Well, you've had a whole week on it. **Emma:** Yeah and if you remember, you didn't give me a straight answer when I asked you how long I had. **Manager:** So how long are you going to be?	**Manager:** So, Emma, what's gone well since last week? **Emma:** Well, I'm about a week ahead of schedule. **Manager:** A week ahead. Wow, how did you do that? **Emma:** I've been asking myself that! I think it was about getting everyone else on board early on. So when I needed anything from any of the others they were ready to deliver.

▶

Emma: I'm not sure. They keep changing their mind about what they want. We didn't have a proper spec at the beginning, remember.

Manager: This is no joke, Emma. This isn't fast enough. I'm going to have Finance breathing down my neck about the costs.

Emma: Well, if you stop breathing down my neck I'll be able to get on with it, won't I!

Manager: Don't let me down, Emma!

Manager: Great. You're such a good influencer, Emma. That's come up quite a few times in our review conversations now, hasn't it?

Emma: Mmm . . . I guess so. I enjoy that a lot. Building the working relationships early on. Getting everyone engaged and on board, and clear about their role.

Manager: You're going to love leading your own team, aren't you? So, getting everyone on board early helped you get a week ahead of schedule. What other positive impacts have come out of this?

Emma: Well, I think we're going to come in under budget. Like we discussed, Ash has helped me do the number crunching. I'll keep you posted but it looks like we'll do it for about 65% of the original budget.

Manager: Terrific. You should be proud of this, Emma. It's great work. And your work on the numbers shows great attention to detail and your ability to stay outcome focused.

Emma: Thanks. It's been fun actually!

Manager: Really? That's great. So what has been enjoyable about it?

Emma: Well, maybe it's that outcome focus and attention to detail you've just mentioned. I get a real buzz out of delivering with all the 'i's dotted and 't's crossed.

Principle 3

Manage weakness from strength. *By always focusing on what works and what people are doing well, I help them find the energy to make things work even better, and to manage their weaknesses from strength.*

My interactions with individuals in one-to-one situations

Weakness focus and problem focus	Strengths focus and solution focus
Manager: Emma, I've just had Finance on the phone, as predicted. They say there are problems with your budget for the Delta Project. **Emma:** God, I hate budgets. **Manager:** Yeah that's all very well, Emma. But the problem is, if you don't mind me saying, that it wasn't done properly. **Emma:** I did do it as carefully as I could. **Manager:** Yeah . . . mmm. Maybe not quite carefully enough, eh? Maybe I should send you on a course. **Emma:** Oh God . . . **Manager:** The thing is, Emma, it's an important part of the job. You need to be good at it. **Emma:** Yeah, OK . . . **Manager:** Meanwhile, it needs sorting out. Send me the file and I'll do it. **Emma:** Oh . . . OK . . . er . . . .thanks. **Manager:** I could really do without this, Emma. I'm busy enough. Make sure everything else in the project is covered properly. OK? I really haven't got the time to have to cover for you on anything else. **Emma:** Sorry . . .	**Manager:** So, Emma, great work on the Delta Project. How on track are you at the moment, on a scale of 1–10? **Emma:** I'd probably give it a 7. **Manager:** And where would you have scored it a week ago? **Emma:** Probably about a 5 and a half. **Manager:** Great, so apart from what you said about getting everyone on board, what else has helped you to get to a 7 now? **Emma:** Mmm . . . let's think . . . Well, I think these regular check-ins with you have helped. You're not involved in the project, so you provide an objective outside view. And I think the regular meetings with the customer service department have helped too. Makes me feel confident that I am heading in the right direction. **Manager:** Great. So you're at a 7. That's pretty impressive. And what stops it being an 8 or a 9? **Emma:** Well, actually I think we could have been two weeks ahead by now. I think the original estimates on how much needed doing were a little generous. So in my mind we could be further forward. I think I let myself down with the number crunching again. Not on the budget – as I said, Ash helped me on that. It was the calculations I did on the IT requirements. They weren't right, and I ended up giving the IT guys the runaround for a few days getting stuff ready that I ended up not needing.

▶

Weakness focus and problem focus	Strengths focus and solution focus
	Manager: So this sounds like a generally weak area for you. As you say, we've discussed it before. None of us are good at everything, are we? So which of those strengths that we identified could help you here?
	Emma: Mmm . . . not sure . . . Well, maybe it's down to my influencing skills again here. What I could have done is go to the IT guys earlier on, and got them to help me put the spec on that together, rather than do it myself.
	Manager: Good idea. And when are you going to need to do that again in the rest of the project?
	Emma: Well, the final implementation after the pilot will involve more spec on IT. Maybe I should get them involved sooner rather than later on that and get them to help me from square one.
	Manager: Great. Anyone else who could support you with this, Emma?
	Emma: Mmm . . . Well, I know that Billy led a large project which had some similarities with this one. Maybe I could pick his brains.
	Manager: Great. Sounds like a good plan, Emma. So how confident are you feeling that you can get fully on track now?
	Emma: Yeah, that's much better. Thanks for that.
	Manager: See you next week. Great work, Emma.

How do I conduct one-to-one conversations with team members which will build confidence, motivation and strength and increase performance?

From these examples you will have got a clear flavour of strengths-focused and solution-focused conversations, and also their opposites – conversations that are weakness-focused and problem-focused.

So, if you want to be having strengths-focused conversations you may now be asking yourself, 'How do I prepare myself? Which questions do I ask? When do I ask them?'

To help you answer these questions in a simple and straightforward way we have organised them into these six conversation areas that as a leader you may often find yourself in:

1. Setting goals
2. Reviewing progress
3. Addressing problems
4. Addressing weaknesses
5. Exploring and shaping further progress
6. Committing to action

We'll now take them one at a time. The following tables show either the question or statement on the left, as well as the purpose or impact of that question or statement on the right. Once again the questions and statements assume a 'coaching' style, where you will encourage the person to come up with their own goals and actions towards them. If you are not clear about when it's best to do this, please read the chapter on strengths-focused coaching (Chapter 11).

 ## Setting goals

Question or statement	Purpose or impact of the question or statement
1. What will success look like?	1. Clear description of success.
2. How will you/we measure it?	2. Ditto.
3. What will be good about achieving it?	3. Enhances motivation.

▶

Question or statement	Purpose or impact of the question or statement
4. When would you ideally like to be there?	4. Puts success within a specific time frame.
5. How clear are you about your role and actions.	5. Clarity on how to achieve success.
6. How confident do you feel about achieving this? (Competence)	6. Measures and develops confidence/competence.
7. How enthusiastic to you feel about your role? (Energy)	7. Measures and enhances motivation/energy.
8. (If needed) How can we increase your clarity, confidence and enthusiasm?	8. Enhances confidence/competence and motivation/energy.
9. How well does your role play to your strengths?	9. Aligns goal with strengths (if these have been identified).
10. How could we make more of your strengths in achieving this goal?	10. Enhances alignment between goal and strengths.
11. What weaknesses might show up that are important?	11. Identifies important weaknesses.
12. How can we manage these best? What strengths can you use to do it?	12. Plan to manage weaknesses.

Reviewing progress

Question or statement	Purpose or impact of the question or statement
1. What has been going particularly well?	1. Clear identification of successes and generation of accompanying energy.
2. How did you achieve this? What were the key elements in succeeding with this?	2. Builds clarity on ingredients for success and builds confidence/competence.
3. What difference has it made? What's been the positive impact?	3. Identifies important details and enhances motivation/energy.
4. What did you particularly enjoy about it?	4. Identifies alignment with strengths and enhances motivation/energy.
5. On a scale of 1–10, how on track are you?	5. Clear measurement to monitor progress now and later.
6. What else has helped you do this well?	6. Identifying important support, resources or strengths.

7. Summarise the above points with: 'So from what you've told me it sounds like you've been really good at . . .' or ' This sounds like another great example of your strength of . . .'.	7. Enhances confidence/competence and motivation/energy.
8. What/who could help you get even further with this?	8. Identifies further relevant support, resources or actions for further success.
9. What strengths do you have that could help?	9. Alignment with strengths.

Addressing problems

Question or statement	Purpose or impact of the question or statement
1. What has been the problem?	1. If needed, allows the person a space to vent.
2. What's been difficult?	2. Ditto.
3. How has this problem impacted you, and others?	3. Ditto, and identifies relative significance of the problem.
4. What has helped you get through it so far?	4. Identifies strengths and resources or relevant support. Enhances confidence.
5. When you have had difficulties like this in the past, what got you through it?	5. Identifies strengths and resources or relevant support. Enhances confidence.
6. If you could remove this problem, how would things ideally be instead?	6. Identifies a clear preferred future/ goal.
7. On a scale of 1–10, how close to that are you now?	7. Clarifies the distance to travel.
8. What progress have you already made?	8. Clarifies distance already travelled. Enhances confidence.
9. How did you achieve this existing progress?	9. Clarifies strengths, resources or relevant support. Enhances confidence.
10. Have you ever been higher on this scale?	10. Identifies any earlier successes/ progress.
11. What was different then? How did you do that?	11. Identifies strengths and resources or relevant support. Enhances confidence/motivation.

▶

Addressing weaknesses

Question or statement	Purpose or impact of the question or statement
1. What has gone less well than you would have hoped?	1. Can identify important performance gaps and motivation issues. May allow useful venting.
2. How do you feel about doing this kind of task? What specifically do you dislike? What aspect of it drains you?	2. May allow useful venting. Identifies draining tasks, i.e. weaknesses.
3. What strengths could you deploy more to improve this situation?	3. Approaches weakness from a strength. Enhances confidence/ energy.
4. What other options do we have for improving this situation?	4. Identifies a range of options to manage a weakness, e.g. role sharing, delegation, upskilling, etc.
5. Who else can help that has relevant skills, knowledge, strengths?	5. Identifies strengths, resources or relevant support of others that could potentially be tapped into.

Exploring and shaping further progress

Question or statement	Purpose or impact of the question or statement
1. What would be the signs of a step forward from where you are now?	1. Clear identification of success criteria for progress. Builds personal ownership of solution.
2. When would you ideally like to be there?	2. Puts success within a specific time frame.
3. What are all the different ways you could get there? What other options do you have?	3. Creates options and therefore more potential to succeed. Builds on personal ownership of solution.
4. What else? (repeat)	4. Stretches thinking beyond the obvious first ideas.
5. What would others say you could do? (Stipulate some key stakeholders in their situation or experts in the field)?	5. Stretches thinking beyond the obvious first ideas. Encourages other perspectives.

6. Which of your strengths could you best deploy here? How would you use it?	6. Explores potential for aligning solutions with strengths. Stretches thinking on options. May enhance confidence/motivation.
7. Would you like some further suggestions from me?	7. Offers any useful ideas, but only after the person has built their own (maintaining personal ownership of solution).

Committing to action

Question or statement	Purpose or impact of the question or statement
1. Which of these options would you like to commit to?	1. Clear identification of preferred options. Builds personal ownership of steps forward.
2. When would you ideally like to have them done by?	2. Puts success within a specific time frame
3. How confident do you feel about getting them done? 1–10?	3. Measures confidence.
4. (If needed) How could you increase your confidence?	4. Enhances confidence.
5. How enthusiastic do you feel about doing these things?	5. Measures motivation/energy/enjoyment.
6. What will be good about doing this?	6. Enhances energy/motivation.
7. (If needed) How could you increase your enthusiasm?	7. Enhances energy/motivation/enjoyment.
8. What support could you get from others?	8. Can enhance confidence.
9. Who else needs to know about your plans?	9. Can enhance support and confidence.

With many skills or approaches it's a question of 'use it or lose it'. So think of a conversation you need to have in the next week where you could have an opportunity to use some of these elements. You could then take a copy of the relevant tables to guide you through the conversation.

As you think about having the conversation, especially if it is with one of your team you have managed for a long period, you may also be asking yourself, 'Won't she think it's strange if I suddenly ask her questions she has never heard me ask before?' This is a good point. With people you know well, you may want to prepare them a little. You could say, 'Look, I've come across some useful questions for us to have a look at. Let me ask you a few and you can let me know how helpful they are.'

Use the following checklist to prepare yourself:

Conversation with... On.................... at.................

We will be:

1. _____ Setting goals

2. _____ Reviewing progress

3. _____ Addressing problems

4. _____ Addressing weaknesses

5. _____ Exploring and shaping further progress

6. _____ Committing to action

Other preparation I need to do:

_____ Copy tables of relevant questions

_____ Explain that I am trying out a new approach

_____ ....

_____ ....

Applying a strengths focus to day-to-day conversations

1. Strengthen your mindset by building the habit of:

   i   starting with an outcome focus;

   ii focusing on what's working;

   iii managing weakness from strength.

2. If you think you are not already doing it, make a habit of focusing on what you want and what's working rather than what you don't want and what's not working.

3. To get the most from one-to-one conversations with your team members, use the six scripts until you can have these types of conversation without them. Download them from our website www.sfleadership.co.uk

Strengths-focused meetings

The greatest ability in business is to get along with others and to influence their actions.
(John Hancock, 18th-century businessman and statesman)

THE SMALLEST AMOUNT OF RESEARCH on the subject of meetings shows fairly quickly that many people have a regular experience of bad meetings. So you're bound to have experienced meetings at which:

▌ people arrive late and leave early;

▌ there are poor objectives, agendas, location information, or conference dial-in information for remote participants;

▌ priorities were not communicated before or during the meeting, leading to focus on less important things;

▌ people were focused on just about everything but the meeting (e.g. email, texts, phone calls, other work on their laptops, doodling);

▌ agreements and actions were not documented, and in many cases meetings ended without assigned responsibilities;

▌ the meeting never gets better. People make the same mistakes every time;

▌ the meeting extended far beyond the allocated time.

In this chapter we'll be looking at the potential a strengths focus has to offer you to have more effective meetings.

By the end of this chapter you will have answers to the following questions:

1   What are the features of meetings which focus on strengths and solutions (as opposed to weaknesses and problems)?

2   How do I incorporate a strengths focus into my own meetings?

What are the features of meetings which focus on strengths and solutions (as opposed to weaknesses and problems)?

We looked at three key principles that come out of a strengths focus (in Chapter 9):

1   Start with an outcome focus.

2   Focus on what's working.

3   Manage weakness from strength.

From the examples and questions related to these three principles you'll have a feel for the type of interactions that are likely in a strengths-focused meeting or team discussion, compared to one which is more weakness- and problem-focused. If you are really keen to get the essence of strengths-focused meetings we would recommend reading Chapter 9 and its examples to bring those principles alive for yourself. In our ideas that follow below, we are also indebted to the great work of Nancy Kline and her seminal book *Time To Think*,[1] which describes very well the characteristics of effective communication in meetings.

The top 10 features of strengths-focused meetings

From our experience of great meetings, here are ten ways to bring a strengths focus to your meetings:

1   Start on a positive.

2   Celebrate and explore successes.

3   Always have an outcome focus.

4   Focus on solution (as opposed to problem).

5   Get from solution to action.

---

1   Kline, N. (1999) *Time to Think: Listening to ignite the human mind*, London, Ward Lock.

6 Get a good balance (between appreciation vs criticism, between asking others for ideas vs telling them yours, and between an inward focus within the team vs an outward focus beyond the team).

7 Listen fully (without interruption).

8 Take turns.

9 End on a positive note and acknowledge contributions.

10 Evaluate.

Here is what each of those means.

Start on a positive

You'll know from what you've read earlier that people are more likely to think better and be more creative if they are in a resourceful state. Starting the meeting with what's positive in people's work helps to create that resourceful state. It also embodies the focus on strength as opposed to weakness. A typical way to start a strengths-focused meeting is to ask each person to share an achievement or success in their work since the last meeting.

Celebrate and explore successes

Following on from the previous point, not only at the beginning of the meeting, but also throughout it, celebrating and exploring how successes were achieved and their impact is very valuable work. It will build a common view of best practice and success, and build the group and each individual's confidence and motivation to achieve it.

Always have an outcome focus

An outcome focus begins well before a meeting, before even the planning stage. It begins when a regular meeting is set up. The questions 'What outcomes do we want from this meeting and how will we know we are succeeding with it?' 'Who needs to attend and why?' are invaluable to develop a clear purpose and terms of reference for the group attending it. To have really effective meetings this purpose will be clear and regularly reviewed.

Asking yourself 'What outcome do I want from this meeting?', 'What outcomes will the other attendees want from this meeting?' and 'What do I want the others to be thinking, feeling or planning to do at the end of our meeting?' are all excellent questions to aid your preparation for a successful meeting. This clarity can then be communicated to attendees with an outcomes-focused agenda. That's an agenda that lets attendees know what the desired outcome is for each slot, not just the topic of discussion. That way they can also prepare themselves better.

At the meeting itself, this outcome focus can also be built as a regular habit by starting the meeting with checking what outcomes each of the attendees wants from the meeting, and then keeping focused on them throughout the meeting. This allows everyone present to monitor the progress of the meeting towards its stated outcomes, as well as the relevance of anything being done or discussed.

Focus on solution (as opposed to problem)

As any challenge, issue or problem is explored or discussed, a solution focus will mean that the focus of the discussion will be about what we want (solution), and how we can achieve it, rather than what we don't want (problem) and what or who is causing it. It also means that if we are focused on what we want, we are also keen to know 'What progress have we already made?', 'How did we do that?' and 'When have we achieved this or something like it in the past, how did we do it?' These questions focus the group on what works, and on their strengths.

Get from solution to action

Later (in Chapter 11, on strengths-focused coaching) we will introduce you to the tried and tested GROW model of coaching. Although originally a process for one-to-one coaching the model also works very effectively as a structure for moving from problem to solution to action in a meeting.

Get a good balance (appreciation vs criticism, ask vs tell, and inward vs outward focus)

Losada and Heaphy[2] studied the nature of communication in business teams' meetings. They found the following in high-performing teams, as opposed to medium- or low-performing teams.

---

[2] Losada, M. and Heaphy, E. (2004) 'The Role of Positivity and Connectivity in the Performance of Business Teams: A nonlinear dynamics model', *American Behavioral Scientist* 47, pp. 740–65.

	Low performing	Medium performing	High performing
Ratio of appreciation to criticism	0.4:1	2:1	6:1 up to 11:1
Ratio of advocacy (promoting my ideas) to enquiry (asking others for their ideas)	0.1:1	0.7:1	1:1
Ratio of focus on self (me, my team, my organisation) to focus on other (person or team in other departments or organisations)	0.01:1	0.6:1	0.9:1

Put in everyday language, individuals in less effective teams tend to criticise much more than they appreciate, put forward their own ideas much less than ask about or listen to those of others, and focus on their own concerns with very little focus on the concerns of their stakeholders. In high-performing teams, on the other hand, we are likely to find individuals who appreciate one another much more than they criticise, and have a fairly equal balance between putting forward their own ideas and asking for and listening to the ideas of others. They also tend to have a fairly equal balance between a focus on their own concerns and a focus on the concerns of their stakeholders beyond the team.

In a strengths-focused team you can encourage these good habits by asking, 'What's good about that idea or contribution?', 'What does everyone else think?', 'What other ideas do we have about this?' and 'What will our customers, suppliers, other departments think about this?' You can also role model the behaviours by offering positive feedback, listening to the views of others well, and showing that you value the perspectives of the range of stakeholders of the team or group.

Listen fully (without interruption)

One way to encourage the appreciation we have just mentioned is to ensure that we listen well to one another. A team or regular meeting can set its ground rules to create an expectation that we have one speaker at a time, and that each speaker speaks without interruption. We have occasionally helped groups who struggle with this one by introducing a 'talking pen' – only the person holding the pen is allowed to speak.

Take turns

Nancy Kline, the writer mentioned previously, suggests that if there is one place to start in improving the quality of a meeting it is by instituting what she terms 'rounds'. This is where the group is presented with a question in relation to an agenda item and each person takes a turn to answer it. We have used this technique with many groups and teams and found it an invaluable method for helping teams and groups to really listen to one another and value each different perspective.

End on a positive note and acknowledge contributions

A strengths-focused ending will obviously be about looking at questions like 'What have we achieved in this meeting?' It can also be about acknowledging individual contributions. We sometimes ask meeting participants to end by mentioning one particular contribution of the person to their left that they have appreciated. This obviously encourages a sense of being valued for each individual, as well as positively reinforcing the behaviours and 'strengths' that make the meeting successful, thus making them more likely to happen again in the future.

Evaluate

Building on the previous point, we always make the habit of asking groups and teams two simple evaluative questions at the end of every meeting. These are:

▌ What was good about this meeting?

▌ How could we make it even better next time?

We would very much encourage this habit with anyone wanting to run highly effective meetings. The habit creates an enormously useful cycle of continuous improvement, as well as an atmosphere which welcomes well-constructed (and strengths-focused) feedback.

The GROW model in meetings

As mentioned, in the next chapter we will explore in some detail how you can coach individuals in your team using a strengths-focused version of the GROW model. Here is how that GROW model process can be used in meetings. Using this structure will help you put in place many of the features mentioned above.

You can use the model in meetings when any agenda item needs a clear goal as well as an action plan towards it.

The GROW model in meetings

Goal

1. What would success look like in relation to this situation?
2. How will we measure our success in a way that is specific, measurable, achievable, realistic and time framed?
3. What would be good about achieving this, for others and for us?

Reality

1. Where are we on a 1–10 scale, where 10 is us having succeeded with the goal?
2. Have we been lower? What progress have we already made? How did we do that?
3. What resources do we have available to us? (time, money, people, skills, knowledge)
4. What obstacles might there be to us moving ahead?
5. When have we succeeded in situations like this in the past? How did we do it?

Options

1. What would be the signs of us moving up 1 point on this scale? Where do we want to be with this by our next meeting?
2. What are all the different things we might do before our next meeting that would move us a step forward?
3. What else? (Brainstorm?) And what else? (getting multiple options)
4. Who are our key stakeholders? What would they say we could do to take a step forward?

Way forward

1. Which of these actions do we definitely want to commit to? (If it is a majority decision let's vote on it.)
2. Who, what, when? – action plan
3. How enthusiastic do we feel about taking this action?
4. How confident do we all feel that we can definitely get this done in the time scale discussed?

Working through this structure will give you opportunities to instigate turn taking without interruptions, when you need to explore any important question in detail, and to gather a variety of different views.

Reviewing the progress of a previously set goal in a strengths-focused way will incorporate the ROW of the GROW model, since the Goal will already have been set at the initial discussion. The Reality stage could incorporate the following:

ROW to review progress

Reality

1. What successes or achievements have we had on this since our last meeting?

2. How did we achieve this? What was the impact?

3. What else?

   (Lots of opportunities here to celebrate and explore individual and collective success and achievements. This allows an ongoing process of identifying strengths, and building a common view of best practice. It also positively reinforces helpful behaviours, and builds confidence and motivation.)

4. What strengths did we show/develop in this piece of work?

5. What didn't go so well? What do we usefully learn from that? What strengths/skills/knowledge would have helped us succeed? Where do we have them in the team? How can we develop them more? Who has the best natural fit for that?

6. Where are we now on our 1–10 scale, where 10 is us having succeeded with the goal?

7. What obstacles might there be to us moving ahead?

8. When have we succeeded in situations like this in the past? How did we do it?

We would recommend reading the next chapter on strengths-focused coaching if you would like to gain further understanding of the GROW model and its strengths-focused applications.

How do I incorporate a strengths focus into my own meetings?

We now lay out a plan for what you can do before, during and after a meeting to build a strengths-focused meeting culture in your team or group:

Before the meeting

- Have a clearly defined purpose for the meeting, with measurable outcomes, and a group of attendees who each has a specific and valuable contribution to make.
- Decide on the outcomes this meeting needs to achieve for you and for others.
- Review the record of the last meeting to see which items need revisiting. In addition, review the evaluation of the last meeting to see how to improve this one.
- Construct an outcomes-focused agenda.

At the start of the meeting

- Begin by saying, 'Let's take a turn to say one important achievement we've made since our last meeting.'
- Then say, 'Let's take a turn to say what we each want to get from this meeting.'

Working with any new challenge, goal or issue

- Use the four stages of the GROW model to find a way forward with this situation.

Reviewing progress on any previously agreed goals and actions

- Use the three stages of the ROW from the GROW model to review progress, what we learn from it, and what are our next steps.

At the end of the meeting

- Ask, 'What have we achieved today?'

Evaluation

▌ Ask, 'What went well in this meeting?'

▌ And finally ask, 'How can we make the next one even better?'

After the meeting

▌ Promptly send out a record of the meeting which lists the key outcomes, actions, achievements and evaluation. This will support the attendees to succeed with their actions, and will also inform the agenda for the next one.

In the next chapter we will explore strengths-focused coaching in its application to one-to-one conversations. We consider the ability to coach in this way as a must in the toolkit of a strengths-focused leader. So read on.

ACTION POINTS

Strengths-focused meetings

1 Have a copy of the 10 features of strengths-focused meetings to hand at each team meeting:

  i   Start on a positive.

  ii   Celebrate and explore successes.

  iii   Always have an outcome focus.

  iv   Focus on solution (as opposed to problem).

  v   Get from solution to action.

  vi   Get a good balance (between appreciation vs criticism, between asking others for ideas vs telling them yours, and between an inward focus within the team vs an outward focus beyond the team).

  vii   Listen fully (without interruption).

  viii   Take turns.

  ix   End on a positive note and acknowledge contributions.

  x   Evaluate:

    a   What was good about this meeting?

    b   How could we make it even better next time?

2 Use the strengths-focused version of GROW model as an effective problem-solving, or solution-creating, tool.

3 Use ROW to review progress on previously set goals.

4 Follow the suggestions for actions before and after the meeting.

Strengths-focused coaching

Leaders don't create followers, they create more leaders.
(Tom Peters, business management author)

THIS IS NOT A BOOK ABOUT COACHING. It is a book about developing yourself as a strengths-focused leader. So why do we have a chapter on coaching?

Well, we would argue that a strengths-focused leader does what Tom Peters, the business writer, describes in our quote above.

There are many ways to build people's strengths, their confidence, their motivation, their initiative and their leadership. An important one of these is coaching.

By the end of this chapter you will have answers to the following questions:

1 What is coaching and what are its specific benefits?
2 When should I coach and when should I not?
3 How do I coach in a strengths-focused way?

What is coaching and what are its specific benefits?

You may be familiar with coaching already, either from being on the receiving end, or from the experience of being a leader who coaches others, or perhaps from previous training or learning on the topic.

If you have had no contact with coaching as yet, perhaps we should give a fairly simple definition:

> Coaching is an interaction that draws out the solutions and ideas of the person being coached in order to maximise their performance and engagement at work.

You'll see from this definition that it is very different from what you sometimes have to do as a leader or manager, which is to tell people what to do. Coaching involves asking your team member what they think their goal is and how they see themselves achieving it.

If you haven't come across coaching before you may be wondering if there is anything of real value to you in it. Is it the latest HR fad or does it make a real difference? Well, in the last 15 years or so since it has had a growing presence in the workplace, research has already shown that coaching can:[1]

For the coachee:

▌ improve performance;

▌ develop more effective use of skills and abilities;

▌ increase job satisfaction and motivation.

For the coaching leader:

▌ achieve improved communication;

▌ increase staff involvement;

▌ aid more effective delegation;

▌ help develop more effective teams;

▌ achieve higher levels of performance.

When we are training leaders in how to coach someone will often ask, 'Which of these is the best approach – telling or asking (coaching)?' Well, if you've been around as a leader for a while you may already know the answer – it all depends!

---

[1]   Fielden, D. S. (2005) *Literature Review: Coaching effectiveness – a summary. A summary of a report for the NHS Leadership Centre by Dr Sandra Fielden of Centre for Diversity and Work Psychology,* Manchester Business School, University of Manchester. Research into Leadership, Modernisation Agency Leadership Centre.

When should I coach and when should I not?

So when should you tell rather than ask? This is our view.

Tell approach

I have the relevant skill/knowledge about this situation and they don't. They need me to show them.
They are new to the job and don't know enough yet to answer any questions about the job.
There is no choice about this. It has to be done this way. A law, policy, etc. says so.
This is a high-risk decision. I have to take it, not them.
There is no time to ask about their ideas, it has to be done right now, this way.
I have explored their ideas as far as possible. Nothing came of it, and we need to get on now.

When we train leaders to coach, we often ask them, 'So if those are the situations when you ought to "tell", when then should you "ask"?' The answer we often get is: 'The rest of the time!' More specifically the time to 'ask' is:

Ask approach

The person I manage has the necessary skill and knowledge to work this out for themselves.
This person keeps coming to me for answers. I think they are ready now to find their own answers and build up some autonomy.
I have been promoted to the level where I actually don't know the detail of what they do. They are the ones with the answers to their problems, not me.
This is a situation where it is fine, and best, for this person I manage to choose their own way to do it.
It is safe for the person to make their own decision here.
There is enough time for them to work out their own answer to this, and it would be good for their development to take the initiative on this.
I haven't explored their ideas, and that is worth doing.
I want to help this person to develop themselves, to take more initiative, and to build their confidence.
I want to make this person less dependent on me, and be able to be more self-reliant. (This will save me time too!)

Exercise: ask v tell

It may be worth taking a moment to reflect on your own balance between 'asking/coaching' and 'telling' and what you would like it to be.

Current balance		Ideal balance	
Asking/Coaching:	%	Asking/Coaching:	%
Telling:	%	Telling:	%

Our experience of doing this self-assessment with leaders is that they are often very familiar with how to do the 'tell', and do lots of it (!). They are much less clear on when they should coach and how to do it, and they realise that they don't do enough of it.

We'll now explain how you can do more coaching, and do it in a way that builds on all that we have done in the book so far. Here is how you coach in a strengths-focused way.

How do I coach in a strengths-focused way?

There are many different psychological models that have been applied to coaching. You can find coaches who do cognitive behavioural coaching, gestalt coaching, NLP coaching, and psychodynamic coaching, to name but a few. So what is strengths-focused coaching? Our guess is that if you have read all of the previous chapters you will already have a good idea about the answer to that question. We described strengths-focused and solution-focused conversations in a work context (in Chapter 9). Leaders engaged in these types of conversations operate from a strengths-focused mindset. This mindset will create conversations which exhibit three key principles:

1. Start with an outcome focus.
2. Focus on what works.
3. Manage weakness from strength.

We also gave detailed examples of conversations which are strength- and solution-focused, and compared them to those that are more weakness- and problem-focused (in Chapter 9). So applying these characteristics to coaching we would define strengths-focused coaching as:

> Coaching which enables the coachee to more effectively achieve their goals by focusing on building on success and strength (as opposed to focusing on problems and fixing weaknesses).

So if you are clear about what strengths-focused coaching is, is there any evidence that it will work for you? We know from the evidence we outlined previously (in Chapter 1) that, where managers and leaders focus on the strengths of their employees, there is increased performance and engagement. Coaching then is a tool to have those conversations that focus on strengths and potential rather than problem, weakness and deficit. Some very recent research has also shown that a solution-focused approach in coaching achieved stronger results than a problem-focused approach.[2]

You may already know how to coach and you may already be doing it. If you have used some of the conversation tools we have outlined (in Chapter 9) then you are definitely coaching already. Often people are already unconsciously using elements of coaching in their work. The trick is to be more consciously aware of what coaching is and how to do it, so that you can make a conscious choice about when to use it, and when not to.

If you are new to coaching we would recommend attending some training that will allow you to practise the skills and tools and get feedback on your use of them. Ask someone you trust to recommend a trainer. This is the quickest and most effective way to learn a skill, rather than read it from a book. What we have written in this chapter, and our video clips (at www.sfleadership.co.uk), will support that learning.

We presented a structure (in Chapter 9) for doing the following in one-to-one strengths-focused conversations:

1. setting goals;
2. reviewing progress;
3. addressing problems;
4. addressing weaknesses;

---

[2] Grant, A. M. (2012) 'Making Positive Change: A randomized study comparing solution-focused vs. problem-focused coaching questions', *Journal of Systemic Therapies* 31 (2), pp. 21–35.

5 exploring and shaping further progress;

6 committing to action.

The good news is that these are also elements of coaching conversations. In fact a coaching session is often made up of a number of these elements. We can put them together into an overall structure or model for the conversation. There are a number of coaching models which supply this kind of structure. By far the most popular one is the simple yet powerful GROW model,[3] developed by Graham Alexander, Alan Fine and Sir John Whitmore.

Many of the other coaching models are subtle variations of GROW.

The GROW model supplies the following four-stage structure to the coaching conversation:

G Goal	What outcome are you aiming for?
R Reality	What progress have you already made towards it, and what obstacles might there be to overcome?
O Options	What are all the things you could do as a step forward?
W Way forward	What actions will you take?

You'll see that the model incorporates elements of our six tools:

1 setting goals;

2 reviewing (*existing*) progress;

3 exploring and shaping further progress;

4 committing to action.

These four simple steps of the GROW model can be developed and expanded in many ways. In the last chapter we presented its application within team meetings. What we will outline here is a strengths-focused version of GROW as it is applied to one-to-one discussions. When employing it we may use some or all of the following questions:

---

[3] Alexander, G. (2006). 'Behavioural Coaching: The GROW Model', in J. Passmore, ed., *Excellence in Coaching: The industry guide*, London, Kogan Page, pp. 61–72.

Strengths-focused GROW

G Goal	1. What will success look like? 2. How will you/we measure it? 3. What will be good about achieving it? 4. When would you ideally like to have achieved it? 5. How confident do you feel about achieving this? (Competence) 6. How enthusiastic do you feel about this goal? (Energy) 7. (If needed) How can we increase your confidence and enthusiasm?
R Reality	8. On a scale of 1–10 where are you now, if 10 is the achievement of the goal? 9. What progress have you already made? How did you achieve this? What were the key elements in the success so far (identifies strengths)? 10. Have you ever been higher on the scale? What was different then? 11. What could help you get even further with this? 12. What strengths have you used so far that will be useful later?
O Options	13. What would be the signs of a step forward from where you are now? 14. What are all the different ways you could get there? What other options do you have? 15. What else? (repeat, repeat?) 16. What would others say you could do? (Stipulate some key stakeholders in their situation or experts in the field)? 17. Which of your strengths could you best deploy here? How would you use it? 18. What has helped in situations like this in the past? 19. Would you like some further suggestions from me?
W Way forward	20. Which of these options would you like to commit to? 21. When would you ideally like to have them done by? 22. How confident do you feel about getting them done? 1–10? 23. (If needed) How could you increase your confidence? 24. How enthusiastic do you feel about doing these things? 25. What will be good about doing this? 26. (If needed) How could you increase your enthusiasm? 27. Who else needs to know about your plans? 28. What support could you get from others? Who else has relevant skills, knowledge, strengths?

To see this coaching model put into practice visit our website at www.sfleadership.co.uk

Here is a short, simple example to show what GROW looks like in practice, using just a few of the questions listed. This is an edited-down version of a conversation that I (Mike) recently had with a coachee. We'll call him George. He had been telling me that he wanted a better work–life balance.

At the front of the coaching session I asked George what he would like to get from the session, so that we had a goal for the coaching session, as well as a goal for his future work-life balance. Having this goal for the session helps George and me to be clear about where we are going in the conversation, and to track our progress. We can call this the 'contracting' around the session.

In the real world . . .

Contracting for the session	**Mike:** So George, if we focus on your work-life balance for the next half-hour, what would you like to get from our discussion? **George:** I've been thinking about this quite a bit over the weekend. And from our session today, I'd like to come away with an action plan that will definitely improve my work–life balance. **Mike:** That's very clear. Let me write that down and we can remind ourselves of that at the end.
G Goal	**Mike:** So what will success look like for you when you get your work–life balance the way you want it, George? **George:** Well . . . I'd be working less hours. I'd be doing 45 maximum, instead of the 70 that's been my habit for the last year or two. Also I'd be leaving at 5.30 pm at the latest every day. And 5 pm on Fridays. Oh and I'd be using that extra time to do 30 minutes at the gym on the way home. And when I got home, I'd be doing the bedtime stories with Jess and Paul. And I would only be doing work at the office. No more than an hour a week at home. That would make such a difference to the weekends. That all might sound ambitious. I know I won't achieve all of that overnight, but I'd like to have all that in place in the next three months. I know you coaches like a time frame!

▶

R Reality	**Mike:** We do! That's great. Very specific and clear ideas about what you want, George. And on a scale of 1–10, where 10 is you having achieved all of this and 1 is you on the starting blocks, where are you today? **George:** Mmm . . . I think I'd say a 3. **Mike:** OK, a 3. So you've made some progress already? **George:** Yeah. I've been talking it through with Beth, my wife. I've already left at 5.30 pm every day this week so far. **Mike:** Wow, that's great, George. And have you ever been higher than a 3 in the past? **George:** Yeah, I have, but that was when I started the job three years ago. **Mike:** And what was different then? **George:** Well, that's simple. I had less work. **Mike:** I see.
O Options	**Mike:** So what would be the signs for you of being at a 4 instead of a 3? **George:** Well, when I think of the answer I've just given, I think it'll be about reducing my workload. **Mike:** Great. So what are all the different ways that could happen? **George:** Well, I can have a session with my boss. I don't think I educate her enough about what my workload and priorities are. Then I end up taking on things that I don't have the time to do properly. **Mike:** And what else might help reduce the workload? **George:** Mmm . . . well, I could delegate more to my team. I got some 360 feedback six months ago and they said they'd like me to delegate more to them. It would develop them more. **Mike:** I see, so they'd like that too. And what else? **George:** I think it would be good to do an Annual Plan for the team. They can be involved. So can my boss. Then we can all be on the same page about creating a realistic and achievable amount across the year. It would also focus us more and make us more effective. We're probably wasting time on less important things at the moment because we haven't got a common view of the priorities. **Mike:** That's really good, George. And which of the strengths that we identified at our last session will help you achieve this? **George:** Well, it's got to be Results Focus, hasn't it? Once I've committed to making it happen, I know I'll really get a buzz out of seeing it through. **Mike:** I'm sure you will!

W Way forward	**Mike:** So, thinking about that Results Focus of yours, George, what exactly do you want to commit to? **George:** Actually now that I think about it, the last idea I had about the Annual Plan is the place to start, because if I do that one, I think it will pick up the other two along the way. My boss's involvement will keep her clear on my workload and priorities, and my team's involvement can include agreeing who is going to take on the different tasks. **Mike:** And when will be the best time for you to get started on this? **George:** Well, I can check my boss's diary this afternoon and put a date in there for around a fortnight's time. **Mike:** Sounds good, George. And how confident are you that this will happen before we meet next month? **George:** Totally. As you know, that Results Focus of mine means I'll be like a dog with a bone until it gets done.
Evaluating the Session	**Mike:** Brilliant. So at the beginning of the session, George, you said you wanted to come away with an action plan that will definitely improve your work–life balance. How well have we done on that? **George:** Very well. It's helped me be really clear about what I want and what I'll do to get it. And I realised that a better work–life balance will also mean better results at work for me and the team. **Mike:** And what could we have done to make the session even better for you? **George:** I'm not sure. Let me think about that. **Mike:** OK, fine. We can check on that when we next meet. Good luck!

This is a short example, to give you the feel for what the GROW model, and a strengths-focused version of it, looks like. A longer conversation would involve using more of the questions shown above. George was very clear on what his goal was. Other people might need more help to clarify exactly what their goal is and how they will measure their success in achieving it. It could also involve more exploration of the obstacles George might meet along the way to his goal, how he will deal with them, what strengths he'll use, and what weaknesses he might need to manage.

The GROW model shown above is ideal when you are having a conversation about setting a goal, and the actions towards it. Once you have set that goal, the next conversation or coaching session you have with the person may be about reviewing progress to that goal, rather than setting a new goal. So the conversation structure will be slightly different. A straightforward way to think of the difference is that the conversation has the same structure, minus the first step – the G or Goal. The second step (Reality) incorporates a review of progress and looks like this:

Progress Review Coaching (ROW)

| Reviewing progress (reality) | 1. What successes have you had so far on this?
2. What did you do to get that success?
3. What are you pleased about?
4. What else? (Repeat till all successes are covered.)
5. What have been the benefits of these successes?
6. Who else has noticed? What would they say has been the positive impact? (Opportunity for positive feedback.)
7. What was your goal? (Set at the first coaching session on this topic.)
8. Scale of 1–10? Where are you now?
9. Where were you last time?
10. What else has helped you progress?
11. Have you been higher? What was different?
12. What has not gone so well?
13. What do you learn from that?
14. What strengths have you used so far that will be useful later? |

You'll find an example of this Progress Review Coaching on our website www.sfleadership.co.uk.

So we invite you to think about how you will develop your coaching approach in your work. Think of the next month. Who can you use this approach with and what type of conversation will it be? As we mentioned (in Chapter 9), if this is someone who knows you well, and may be surprised by your change of style, you may want to prepare them by introducing this new approach, for example by saying, 'I've been looking at doing our conversation in a different way. I have some questions that I think will be useful. You can let me know how it works for you.'

Strengths-focused coaching

1. Create a regular diary slot for each member of your team. This will make coaching a regular habit and more strongly embed the tool and its behaviours.

2. Download our two coaching scripts (Strengths-Focused GROW and Progress Review Coaching) from our website at www.sfleadership. co.uk. Have these with you at each coaching session until you become so familiar with them that you don't need them any more.

Employee processes

A good boss makes his men realize they have more ability
than they think they have so that they consistently
do better work than they thought they could.
(Charles Erwin Wilson, former US Secretary of Defence)

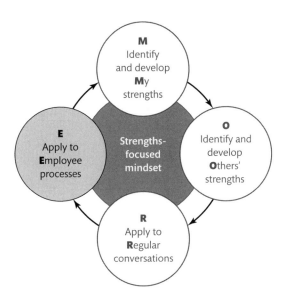

The final '**E**' of the **MORE** model stands for '**E**mployee processes'.

If you have been convinced that strengths-focused leadership can have
a hugely positive impact upon you and your team, we anticipate that
you will be ready to explore how the strengths philosophy and principles

can be incorporated into all the employee processes that exist in your organisation. You may be beginning to ask questions such as:

▌ How can I carry out strengths-focused annual reviews or performance appraisals? (Chapter 12)

▌ How can I have strengths-focused development discussions? (Chapter 13)

▌ How can I incorporate a strengths focus into our recruitment procedures? (Chapter 14)

In the following three chapters we will offer you some suggested approaches for addressing the above questions.

We have found that rather than impose a prescribed strengths-focused solution for all the different employee processes that exist in organisations, it is much more effective to allow those who are responsible for the development and maintenance of such processes to 'strengthen' their own systems and methodologies in a way that feels right for them and their organisation. The size of your organisation, the type of business you are in, the existing processes you have already developed – all of these factors will influence your thinking about how best to strengthen your processes. So, read on, and use our suggestions to develop your own thinking about how best to incorporate strengths into your existing employee processes.

Strengths-focused performance appraisals

Outstanding leaders go out of their way to boost the self-esteem
of their personnel. If people believe in themselves,
it's amazing what they can accomplish.
(Sam Walton, businessman and entrepreneur)

PERFORMANCE APPRAISALS are a very good starting point for incorporating a strengths focus into employee processes. Sometimes referred to as performance reviews, this is the process of having a one-to-one conversation to review *what* your team member has achieved, for example last year's performance against previously agreed objectives and measures, and *how* they have achieved it. This provides the foundation for agreeing performance goals for the forthcoming period.

Often the organisation's values and behaviours provide the basis of the 'how' discussion, but when you are taking a strengths focus, this is a perfect opportunity to explore how strengths have been applied to successes and achievements and how they might be utilised in future objectives. By making some small adjustments to the way you conduct your appraisal conversations you can introduce those being reviewed to the energising and positive impact of focusing on strengths.

If you have already been having regular strengths-based conversations with your team, and if you have already been helping people identify the strengths that will help them achieve their goals and tasks, then you will find it easy to undertake a strengths-focused appraisal.

By the end of this chapter you will have answers to the following questions:

1 Why take a strengths focus in performance appraisal discussions?

2 What does a strengths-focused performance appraisal look like?

3 How can I make the appraisal a positive and motivating experience?

Why take a strengths focus in performance appraisal discussions?

There are many good reasons for carrying out appraisal discussions. Taking time out with your team members to discuss performance as part of an appraisal provides you with an effective means of setting goals and reviewing performance and it also:

▌ demonstrates your commitment to a high-performance culture and continuous learning;

▌ ensures a consistent approach towards managing and assessing performance;

▌ enables regular discussions about performance and progress between you and your team members;

▌ provides clarity to individuals about role, expectations, measures of success and perceived effectiveness;

▌ enhances employee engagement, job satisfaction and performance;

▌ ensures that your team goals are delivered as a result of aligned individual goals.

These all sound like great outcomes for you as a leader, so what else can a strengths-focused approach add to the appraisal process to make it even more effective, engaging and motivating? Empirical research about the impact of focusing on strengths indicates that some of the additional benefits to be gained from focusing more on strengths than on weaknesses include:

▌ A more energising and motivating discussion: because of the focus on the individual's successes and how they have achieved them, including how they have been able to use their strengths. More openness to discuss what didn't work so well and address weaknesses: as a result of the energy created by the strengths focus.

▌A higher level of engagement and motivation to achieve goals: as a result of aligning goals with the individual's strengths, giving them an opportunity to do what they do best in their day-to-day work. (See Chapter 5 for more on how to set strengths-focused objectives.)

▌A higher level of creative thinking: as a result of the positive mindset created.

(See Chapter 1 for more details about the research underpinning a strengths approach.)

What's the evidence?

We have mentioned before one particular study that indicates that focusing on strengths enables higher performance, while focusing on weaknesses can undermine performance. As a reminder, the Corporate Leadership Council research[1] found that taking a strengths focus within appraisal discussions led to improved productivity and engagement. This study found that an emphasis on performance strengths was linked to a 34 per cent improvement in performance. This compared to an emphasis on performance weaknesses that led to a 26.8 per cent decline.

What does a strengths-focused performance appraisal look like?

In strengths-focused appraisals there is a clear shift away from a deficit or weakness focus. There is also a need for you to be genuinely interested in your team member: their lives, their career and their strengths. However, there is no single 'correct' way to ensure your appraisal process is strengths-based. We have worked with organisations that are introducing a strengths-based approach into their way of working, and each approach has to be unique, based upon the needs, existing processes, culture, etc. The different approaches include:

▌Revise your existing appraisal process. This can be a way of introducing various strengths-focused elements, such as a strengths assessment and different ways to capture strengths on the documentation. It can also include strengths-focused questions for team members to use in their preparation and for managers to use in the actual appraisal meeting.

[1] Corporate Leadership Council (2002) *Performance Management Survey*, Washington, DC.

▌ Introduce a new appraisal process. This can include the above elements and incorporate a strengths focus into the training for managers, as well as in the documentation itself.

▌ Leaders adopt a strengths focus in their own way. Having signed up to the strengths-focused mindset and having started to lead with a strengths focus in a range of interactions with the team, leaders often then add a strengths flavour to the appraisal discussions.

What about the paperwork?

Leaders who want to carry out strengths-focused appraisals sometimes believe they are limited by existing documentation. However, the success of any performance review and objective-setting discussion is dependent much more upon the way it is conducted by the leader, than the documentation supporting the process. The remainder of this chapter will focus on what you can do to adopt a strengths focus in your appraisal discussions, even if you are working with existing appraisal processes prevalent in your organisation.

Ten suggestions for strengths-focused appraisals

Here are a number of pointers for your appraisal meetings:

1. Accentuate the positive – but don't ignore the negative.
2. Start on a positive note.
3. Brief your team members, stressing the importance of focusing on what is working and on strengths.
4. Carry out a strengths assessment.
5. Talk about how strengths have been applied to achievements.
6. Review behaviours – how things have been achieved.
7. Agree objectives that are aligned with strengths.
8. Identify development needs that are based on strengths to support achievement of objectives.
9. Discuss career aspirations.
10. Use strengths-based questions throughout.

Accentuate the positive – but don't ignore the negative

▍**Be mindful about focusing on strengths as opposed to weaknesses.**
Your team members cannot tap into their potential with a weakness-focused, negative mindset; they have to use their strengths. Focusing on weaknesses will be de-motivating and put your team member in a less resourceful state.

▍**Focus first on strengths.** This will have an energising effect on both you and your team member. The aim is to focus on what has led to success and how this can be built upon, and how strengths have and can be brought out to play.

▍**Do not ignore negative aspects and what might impede progress.**
Address significant weaknesses, but do not focus on weaknesses at the expense of helping people identify the positive resources they have within them that will help them perform better.

▍**Let people embrace strengths at their own pace.** It is easy for you to become enthusiastic about strengths, especially when you see the evidence in support of taking a strengths approach and when you feel it is aligned with your own philosophy. Others might be a bit more sceptical. However, by merely shifting the focus of attention to what is working and what is energising, but not exclusively, the right balance for each individual can be found, rapport will be built, and individuals are likely to learn the value of focusing on strengths very quickly.

Start on a positive note

▍**Talk about general achievements at the start.** This starts the conversation on a positive note and begins to build the rapport necessary for a productive conversation.

▍**Ask people to prepare their thoughts about what has gone particularly well for them during the year.** You can discuss these overall achievements before you begin diving into a review of what has been achieved against specific objectives. When people think about what has gone particularly well for them during the year, what comes to mind might not necessarily be linked to their objectives. For example, it might be that there has been a lot of change and they believe that they have adapted well to all the changes.

▍**Explore what they did that led to the success.** This serves two purposes: first, it raises their awareness of what they did that led to high performance so that it can be repeated in the future. Secondly, it can highlight an individual's strengths. In the above example, the individual might be able to identify strengths in adapting flexibly to change.

▌ **Offer your overall feedback on what you think the individual has done well.** This is also a great opportunity for you to call out any strengths that you have noticed the individual using during the year that have led to success and high performance.

Brief your team members, stressing the importance of focusing on what is working and strengths

▌ **Introduce the strengths approach.** This is an ideal time to introduce the strengths philosophy and give your team members an opportunity to consider what they like about it, and share any concerns they might have. (See Chapter 6.)

▌ **Brief your team on how to prepare.** Even if your team are on board with the strengths focus, because of people's inherent negativity bias, it is always a good idea to brief people on how you expect them to prepare for their appraisal, and remind them that they will be encouraged to evaluate their own performance, focusing on what is working before considering what is not working so well.

▌ **Offer some questions for reflection.** Questions to reflect on can help prepare people's thoughts. The questions offered later in this chapter are suggestions for you to use in the discussion, but they are equally useful as a framework for both you and your team member to prepare in advance of the appraisal discussion.

Carrying out a strengths assessment

▌ **Use the 5 Step Strengths Map.** If you are using the appraisal process as a way of launching a strengths focus in your team, this is an ideal time to carry out a strengths assessment. This can be done before the appraisal discussion or as part of it, typically after reviewing the previous year's objectives and before reviewing the individual's behaviours or competencies. In this way you can create a link between strengths and competencies and gather some useful information upon which to plan future business goals, behavioural goals and development goals. (See Chapter 3 for how to use the 5 Step Strengths Map.)

▌**Re-visit any previous strengths assessments.** The appraisal discussion is an ideal opportunity to revisit the strengths profile and explore how strengths have been applied and can be applied to maximise performance. (See Chapter 3 for information about the range of assessments available.)

Talk about how strengths have been applied to achievements

▌**Explore how your team member did what they did.** This is one of the easiest ways of bringing a strengths focus to your discussion. You can help your team member explore what has helped their good performance, raising their awareness of their own behaviours that led to success in order that they can do more of it in the future. It is also a very motivating and confidence-building conversation for anyone to have.

▌**Discuss how strengths can be applied in the future.** You can build on the above, exploring what else your team member now knows about their strengths, which can lead into discussions about how they can be applied in the future. Help your team member differentiate between strengths (what they are good at and enjoy) and learned behaviours (what they are good at but actually find quite draining). Reviewing past performance and what individuals have enjoyed/not enjoyed provides some very valuable information to allow individuals to identify their strengths and plan to use them in the future. It will also be a very energising and enlightening conversation, too!

Review behaviours – how things have been achieved

▌**Focus on strengths in relation to competencies.** You may have a framework of values, behaviours or competencies that gives everyone clarity about the behaviours that are required of them to do their job well. To some people, this might appear similar to a dictionary of strengths. What is different, however, is that a competency framework is typically dictating a level to which everyone needs to perform, irrespective of their unique strengths and preferences. Encouraging everyone to be the same and aim for excellence in every competency can actually inhibit high performance. Just think about what happens when an individual puts all their attention on fixing the one or two competencies that fall slightly short of good. Unless these behaviours are significant derailers it is going to be much more beneficial to move the focus of energy to building the competencies that relate to the strengths of the individual so that they stand out for these unique strengths or competencies.

▌**Invite self-evaluation.** Your team member should be encouraged to self-evaluate their own behaviour and think of examples where they have demonstrated the behaviours. A discussion can ensue about whether each behaviour is a strength. You can then discuss your own perception and offer feedback. The aim is to identify areas of good performance and strength and areas where capability can be enhanced.

▌**Link strengths to competencies.** If a strengths assessment has previously been carried out, this is also an opportunity to link the review of the behaviours or competencies to what they know about their strengths.

Agree objectives that are aligned with strengths

▌**Discuss how strengths can be brought to play.** High-quality objectives help people to know what is expected of them and enable people to make a valuable contribution to the organisation at the same time as developing their own capability. When objectives are set, it is a great opportunity to discuss how strengths can be applied to their achievement. (See Chapter 5.)

▌**Coach to build motivation to get started straight away.** If objectives are agreed well, your team members will know exactly what they have to achieve, by when, and to what standard. If you also give some coaching support at the time of agreeing the objective, they will also go away from the review meeting with some clear thoughts about how they can create an action plan to achieve the objective and will be feeling a lot more motivated to get started straight away. (See Chapter 11.)

Identify development needs based on strengths to support achievement of objectives

▌**Notice strengths that can be built upon.** Throughout the appraisal discussion you will be highlighting development needs that can be built into a development plan following the appraisal. As well as identifying gaps or areas that need further development, you will also notice strengths that can be built upon to enable even higher performance, engagement and fulfilment. (See Chapter 13 for how to conduct strengths-focused development discussions.)

Discuss career aspirations

▌**Take time to understand career aspirations.** Having a discussion with your team members about their longer-term career goals enables you to understand some of their motivators, their longer-term plans and how they wish to apply their strengths in the future. You can have a conversation about career development at any time; you don't have to wait until the appraisal discussion.

▌**Encourage openness.** Career discussions need to be open and honest and you need to make sure that your team member feels comfortable discussing any options with you. Having these longer-range discussions can set a meaningful context for shorter-term personal development planning. This can address both longer-term aspirations and job-related shorter-term goals and it is a great opportunity to ensure that career plans and development goals are aligned with the individual's strengths.

Use strengths-focused questions

▌**Give your questions a strengths flavour.** Changing the nature of your questions, ensuring that your team member's strengths are emphasised, creates a very positive shift in the nature of the conversation. Individuals who had previously felt anxious about their appraisal, and worried that it might be a draining conversation focusing on rectifying what they are doing wrong, find that it is the opposite of this: an energising conversation that identifies and builds on what is working and approaches shortfalls from a more positive perspective.

How can I make the appraisal a positive and motivating experience?

To make it easier for you to add a strengths focus to your appraisal discussion and ensure it is a very positive and motivating experience for both you and your team member, we have designed some strengths-focused questions that you might find useful at various stages of the appraisal discussion.

The list of questions that follow is not exhaustive, but merely a starting point for you to take more of a strengths focus in your appraisal discussions.

Questions for a strengths-focused appraisal discussion

Reviewing general achievements

▌ What do you think are the most important achievements in your role this year?

Taking each achievement in turn:

- What was good about achieving that outcome?

- What did you do to get that success?

- What are you particularly pleased about?

- What have you learnt from this?

- What does this success tell you about your strengths? (Opportunity for positive feedback)

Reviewing previous objectives

▌ What was your objective or goal? What were you aiming to achieve?

▌ What were your measures of success?

▌ What have you achieved?

▌ How have you performed against each of the measures?

▌ What has gone well? What are the reasons for this? (Opportunity for feedback)

▌ Which strengths were you able to draw on to help you succeed?

▌ What have you not achieved that you intended to? What are the reasons for this? (Opportunity for feedback)

▌ What could you have done more of/less of/differently to have achieved a better result?

▌ What does this tell you about your strengths, that you can build on next year?

▌ What have you learned?

▌ How will you incorporate this learning into this year's objectives/goals?

▌ What do you need to do now?

Reviewing behaviours (or competencies)

▌ Which behaviours do you demonstrate well?

▌ Do you enjoy using these behaviours? Are they strengths of yours?

▌ What examples have you got of how you demonstrate this behaviour well?

- How has this success affected the results you have achieved?
- What would other people say about your performance in this behaviour?
- How can you build on this behaviour in the future? What would this look like?
- Which behaviours do you think you demonstrate less well?
- What examples have you got of how you demonstrate this behaviour?
- How has this level of success affected the results you have achieved/ not achieved?
- What would other people say about your performance in this behaviour?
- What can you do to turn this around in the future?
- What would this look like?
- What impact would doing this have on your success?

Reviewing career aspirations

- If you could have any job that you want in five years' time what would it be?
- What would you particularly enjoy about it and how would this help you play to your strengths?
- What skills, knowledge and behaviours will you need to have gained to get there?
- What will your ideal job be in two years' time?
- What can you do to develop yourself in that direction?
- What opportunities are there to build the knowledge, skills and behaviours you need for that future role?

Agreeing inspiring performance objectives

- What are you aiming to achieve? For what purpose? In order that what happens? What will success look like?
- What will be good about achieving this objective?
- How will you measure your success? How else?
- Which strengths will you be able to draw on to help you achieve this objective?
- Where are you now in relation to this outcome?

▶

▌ When do you want to have achieved this? What are the milestones along the way?

▌ What ideas have you got for moving forward to achieve this outcome?

Interim/quarterly performance reviews

▌ When have you been at your best over the last three months?

▌ When you were at your best, what did you achieve? How did you make those achievements happen? What has been good about achieving them?

▌ When have you not been at your best? What is the learning from that?

▌ What have you discovered about yourself in the last three months?

▌ What are you looking forward to achieving in the next three months?

▌ Which of your key strengths will you use?

▌ What things are you going to find difficult in the next three months?

▌ How can you plan to use your strengths to address these difficulties?

▌ Which strengths will you align to deliver your goals?

If you are now eager to bring a strengths focus to your appraisal discussions, all the questions above have been incorporated into a template that you can easily use with your team. This template provides you with a ready-made structure for carrying out a strengths-focused performance appraisal. You can use the template to help you and your team member to prepare for the discussion and also to record the outputs from the conversation. To download this template visit our website www.sfleadership.co.uk.

In the real world . . .

We end this chapter with the following example of an organisation incorporating a strengths focus into their appraisal process so you can see what it can look like in reality.

Our client was updating their 'Performance and Development Discussion' (appraisal process), which they saw as an ideal opportunity to introduce managers to the benefits of focusing on strengths. To add a clear strengths focus to their appraisal process, they included a 5 Step Strengths Map exercise as part of both the employee's preparation and the performance discussion itself. All managers attended a briefing to understand the new process and the benefits of taking a strengths approach and to learn how to handle talking someone through their Strengths Map.

In the performance and development meeting, each leader helped their team member explore their strengths. This was done after reviewing the previous year's objectives and before reviewing the individual's behaviours or competencies. In this way, it was possible to create a link between performance, strengths and competencies and provide some useful information upon which to plan future business goals, behavioural goals and development goals. Feedback about the new process has been extremely positive, and it is noticeable how much more people in the organisation are talking about strengths.

ACTION POINTS

Strengths-focused performance appraisals

1. Take a look at your existing performance appraisal documentation. What opportunities do you have to introduce a strengths focus into your existing documents and processes?

2. Decide how you want to incorporate a strengths focus into your appraisals and do the necessary preparation: for example revising the documentation, 'strengthening' the structure of your conversation, becoming familiar with how to use the 5 Step Strengths Map.

3. Ensure your team members are clear about what the 'new' approach to appraisals will look like and what benefits they will get from focusing more on their strengths than their weaknesses.

4. Brief your team about how to prepare for their strengths-focused performance appraisal.

5. Use the 10 tips provided in this chapter to bring a strengths-focused approach to your appraisal discussions. Download the template of questions from our website at www.sfleadership.co.uk

6. Gather feedback from your team members about what they liked about the new approach to appraisal discussions. Ask them what suggestions they have for enhancing the process even further.

13

Strengths-focused development discussions

Treat a man as he is and he will remain as he is. Treat a man as he can and should be and he will become as he can and should be.
(Stephen R. Covey, author)

FOLLOWING ON NATURALLY from the performance appraisal discussions are conversations about development needs and the identification of clear development objectives. In fact, it might be that in your organisation the appraisal process is called 'performance and development discussion' or something similar, emphasising the importance of reviewing previous development goals and agreeing new ones as part of the whole performance management process and doing this alongside the process of reviewing and agreeing business goals.

However, development conversations can happen any time; there is no need to wait for the appraisal discussion. There are many great opportunities for strengths-focused development conversations, including:

▌ regular formal discussions to review progress towards the agreed development goals;

▌ informal check-in conversations between formal reviews;

▌ reviews of development goals that have been achieved and the setting of new ones;

▌ as part of development and training programmes: for example, after a Development Centre.

By the end of this chapter you will have answers to the following questions:

1 Why take a strengths focus in development discussions?

2 What does a strengths-focused development discussion look like?

3 How can I make the development discussion a positive and motivating experience?

Why take a strengths focus in development discussions?

If we were to ask you, 'What outcome do you want from your development conversations?' what would you say? Maybe your responses might include some of the following:

▌ I'd like people to feel engaged and inspired – ready to take action on their development goals.

▌ I'd like people to take complete ownership of their development goals, but know that I'm there to support them.

▌ I'd like people to know that I am interested in their growth and development.

▌ I'd like people to be clear about what they have to do to achieve their development goals.

▌ I'd like people to know that their development plan is focused on developing their strengths – not just focusing on weaknesses.

▌ I'd like people to believe that achieving their development goals will also help them achieve their business goals.

We are sure you will agree that these would be great outcomes, which are all made even more likely when you take a strengths-focused approach to the discussions.

When people hear the words 'development plan', what people typically think of is a plan that is going to address their weaknesses. But, at this stage in the book, you will need no reminding of the energising impact of focusing on building on strengths compared to the draining and de-motivating impact of focusing on weaknesses. Indeed, only significant weaknesses that are seriously impacting your team member's performance need to be addressed within their development plan.

What's the evidence?

We have mentioned already the growing body of evidence that suggests that focusing on strengths (as opposed to weaknesses) in development discussions significantly increases staff performance and engagement. Of particular relevance is:

▮ The Gallup Research[1] and its 12 questions that are used to measure employee engagement. Team members with high Q12 scores exhibit lower turnover, higher sales growth, better productivity, better customer loyalty and other manifestations of superior performance. Of those 12 questions, there are three that are directly and positively impacted by you taking a strengths-focused approach to development discussions. These are:

   - Is there someone at work who encourages your development?

   - In the last six months, has someone at work talked to you about your progress?

   - In the last year, have you had opportunities to learn and grow?

▮ The Corporate Leadership Council found that an emphasis on performance strengths in appraisal, which includes development discussions, was linked to a 36.4 per cent improvement in performance. In contrast, an emphasis on performance weaknesses was linked to a 26.8 per cent decline in performance.[2]

▮ Zenger, Folkman and colleagues'[3] research found that leaders whose development plans were focused on building strengths achieved three times greater improvements in 360 degree feedback ratings than leaders whose development was focused on fixing their weaknesses. The one exception was where there was a significant weakness – this should be addressed as the top priority in development planning.

So, if you want to learn how you can adopt a strengths focus in your development conversations and explore what is different in these conversations, read on.

---

[1] Buckingham, M. and Coffman, C. (2005) *First Break All the Rules: What the world's greatest managers do differently*, London, Simon & Schuster. (Original source: John Thackray, 'Feedback for Real', *Gallup Management Journal*.)

[2] Corporate Leadership Council (2002) *Performance Management Survey*, Washington, DC.

[3] Zenger, J. H., et al. (2012) *How to Be Exceptional: Drive leadership success by magnifying your strengths*, New York, McGraw-Hill.

What does a strengths-focused development discussion look like?

How many of these common mistakes in development planning do you recognise?

▌ You ask someone to come up with their own development plan with no discussion or support.

▌ There are two-word objectives: 'Improve communication', 'Raise profile'.

▌ The objective is set – end of discussion. No discussion about how this goal might be achieved.

▌ The plan focuses on unrealistic or non-guaranteed goals, for example promotion.

▌ The plan focuses only on attending a training course, for example a time management course.

▌ There is a 'cafeteria approach' to development planning, looking at the list of available courses – 'I'll have one of those, and one of those, please'.

▌ The development actions require someone else to take the action or the person expects their manager to 'do' the development 'to them'.

▌ It all seemed like a good idea at the time, but line managers and individuals lose interest over time.

Unfortunately, you will not be on your own if you recognised quite a few of the above.

The key question in development planning

A well-constructed development plan will ensure that your team members grow and develop in a way that positively impacts upon their performance, their behaviours or capabilities, their career plan and the business, too. The key question that a development plan answers is:

> In order to ensure I achieve my current performance objectives and mid-term career aspirations, what do I need to do to develop myself in terms of skill, knowledge or behaviours?

This is not always an easy question for people to answer on their own, and often it is useful to have some coaching support from you as their manager, not only to help them identify their development needs, but also to identify a range of development actions and build their motivation to take these actions.

The 70:20:10 principle

Key to an effective development plan is having a blend of development actions that focus on the individual taking responsibility to perform specific actions to stretch themselves in order to develop, as opposed to merely attending a training course.

The 70:20:10 principle[4] suggests that learning happens in these proportions:

- 70% on-the-job learning via specific job related tasks or projects.
- 20% learning from others such as coaching from a boss, peers, subject matter experts and mentors.
- 10% from formal structured training courses and self-directed learning.

We have found it beneficial to ensure that the blend of development actions within the development plan also follows this ratio. After all, it makes sense that if we are to learn to do something better, we need to find opportunities to put new behaviours into practice through job-related tasks.

In the real world . . .

As an example, Jim was a Senior Manager in an Insurance Company and thought that he could build on his strength of Relationship Builder by building a stronger network inside and outside of the organisation. Did he need to go on a networking course to learn how to do this? Of course he didn't. He just needed to identify opportunities where he would gain personal and business value from widening his network and then take action to set up those opportunities. As a result, he realised that he would develop his networking ability at the same time as enjoying playing to his strengths and it would help him achieve his business goals, too.

What's different in a strengths-focused development conversation?

If you are already having regular development conversations with your team members, and are ensuring that people have development plans that

---

4   Lombardo, M. M. and Eichinger, R. W. (1996) *The Career Architect Development Planner* (1st edn), Minneapolis, Lominger, p. iv.

are being worked on, then it's very easy to make simple changes to ensure that the conversations are strengths-focused.

The main difference is that you will need to ensure that the development goals focus on building on strengths and addressing only significant weaknesses. The conversation will be much more about discussing strengths and opportunities to apply them more in order to enable your team members' strengths to stand out to others and really make a difference to their performance. Even when there are weaknesses to be addressed within the development plan, there is still scope to introduce a strengths focus by exploring strengths that can be drawn upon to address the weakness.

In the real world . . .

Here's an example of the impact that can be achieved by making a simple shift towards a focus on strengths in development planning.

I (Mike) worked with a leadership team in the voluntary sector. As part of the project I did a strengths assessment with each of the six team members. I also asked if I could have a look at their current development plans. I found that all of them had development plans that focused on fixing weaknesses. So, it was no surprise to me to find that none of them had gone very far with their plans. When I worked with them to create development plans based around their strengths the difference was significant. Not only were they very keen to get on with developing their strengths, but the whole team saw a huge increase in effectiveness, morale and energy.

How can I make the development discussion a positive and motivating experience?

Here are some steps that you can take to ensure that your development conversations with your team members are strengths-focused:

1. Capture all the key development areas, focusing on strengths to build on and then prioritise the development areas.

2. Identify desired outcomes or goals for each development area.

3. Identify specific actions that can be taken for each development goal.

4. Review progress regularly and evaluate the impact.

Capture all the key development areas, focusing on strengths to build on

▌ **List the development actions.** Ensure that all the development areas have been captured from the discussions so far, for example if the development plan is being put together following an appraisal discussion, make sure that all the opportunities for building on strengths and also addressing any significant weaknesses have been captured.

▌ **Prioritise the development needs.** It is usual to have three to four development goals where the majority focus is on building existing areas of strengths rather than weaker areas, unless the weakness is critical to performance.

▌ **Focus on the short term.** The development plan does not necessarily have to last all year – as and when the development actions are achieved, they can be reviewed mid-term and new development actions can be agreed. It is much better for the plan to contain actions that can be implemented immediately so that people can have quick wins.

Questions you can ask

What ideas for development have arisen from the performance development discussions so far?

What are some of the key strengths that you would like to build upon as part of your development plan?

What behaviours, values or competencies are in need of development?

What development requirements are necessary to support the achievement of your business objectives for the next period (skill, knowledge or behaviour)?

What development requirements have been discussed in order for you to achieve your career aspirations?

Identify desired outcomes or goals for each development area

▌ **Use the SMARTIE framework.** This will help your team members establish a clear and compelling outcome, including a range of measures of success that can be captured and used to review progress. Time scales are also important.

▌**Be clear if the goal builds on a strength or responds to a weakness.**
It might be that the development goal is directly about building on a
strength, which is great. It could be, however, that the development
goal is about addressing a weakness. If so, it is particularly good to help
your team member explore how they can draw on other strengths to
help them achieve the goal.

Questions you can ask

*For each development area what, specifically, are you looking for as an
end result?*

*What will the measures of success be and when will the targeted results
be achieved?*

*How can you play to your other strengths to help you achieve this
development goal?*

For each development goal, identify specific actions that can be taken

▌**Create a blend of actions.** These actions will include a blend of:

- **Work or job-related opportunities (70%).** What opportunities
  can your team member take as part of their current job role that
  will help them achieve their development need? For example,
  undertaking a piece of work that will exercise the behaviour or skill
  that they want to develop.

- **Manager's/others' support (20%).** What support would your team
  member like to ask for from you and others? For example, coaching,
  mentoring, talking to a colleague, work shadowing, site visits, etc.
  Who else might support?

- **Formal training and self-directed learning (10%).** Is any formal
  training available to support their development need, or is there a
  need for some additional technical training? What other actions or
  activities can they undertake to drive their own development, which
  are not part of their everyday job role? For example, reading books,
  e-learning, self-study.

▌**Identify some first steps.** You can end the development-planning
conversation on a high point by having agreed some initial first steps
that your team member will take to work towards achieving their
development goals straight away.

Review progress regularly and evaluate the impact

▌ **Take a regular interest.** Initiate regular opportunities for your team members to identify and discuss progress they have made. It is so much more motivational to work on a development plan when there is someone else who is really interested in hearing about your achievements! It is also critical to regularly ensure that the development plan is still relevant.

Questions you can ask

What have you achieved that you are pleased about?

How does that progress compare to your plan?

What's been good about the progress you have made?

What does this tell you about your strengths?

What obstacles are preventing your progress, and how can they be eliminated?

What support do you need from me or others?

What additional actions can you take to achieve your goals?

What are your next steps?

 You may have existing frameworks in your organisation that are to be used for development planning. However, if you like the structure we have outlined above go to our website www.sfleadership.co.uk to download a ready-made template with all the useful questions that can help you help others in constructing some compelling and motivational development goals.

ACTION POINTS

Strengths-focused development discussions

1 Take a look at your existing processes for identifying development needs and writing development plans. How strengths-focused are the existing processes?

2 Determine what you need to do to introduce more of a strengths approach to your development conversations.

3 Download the templates on our website for some useful guidance on structure and content of strengths-focused development discussions.

4   Plan in time with each of your team members to either review existing development plans or construct new ones, ensuring that the emphasis is on developing strengths and addressing only significant weaknesses.

5   Practise having some strengths-focused development conversations and notice the results.

6   Review development plans regularly with your team members, emphasising what has been achieved.

Strengths-focused recruitment

*Do not hire a man (or woman) who does your work for money,
but him (or her) who does it for the love of it.*
(Henry David Thoreau, author)

WHEN INCORPORATING STRENGTHS into your organisation's existing
systems and processes, another good place to start can be to look at how
strengths can be embedded into the recruitment process to ensure that
people are offered roles that fit them best, allowing them to play to their
strengths and perform to their full potential.

You will be familiar with the costs of recruiting the wrong person:
low engagement and productivity, disruption to the workflow and the
business, and low team morale, not to mention the time and expense of
the recruitment process itself.

By adopting a strengths focus in your recruitment you can:

▌ let potential new employees know that you are a strengths-focused
organisation;

▌ add energy to the selection process;

▌ gain an early insight about people's strengths and how they are likely to
perform at their best;

▌ select individuals on the basis of what they enjoy doing, and do well, in
order to ensure they are the best fit for the job.

By the end of this chapter you will have answers to the following questions:

1 What does strengths-focused recruitment mean?

2 How do I conduct a strengths-focused interview?

3 How do I prepare to recruit with a strengths focus?

4 What are my next steps?

What does strengths-focused recruitment mean?

There are many different ways that you can incorporate a strengths focus into your recruitment process, ranging from quite simply getting people to discuss their strengths during the interview, through to a more comprehensive strategy for identifying strengths that are essential or preferable for given roles and setting up recruitment processes that enable a team of assessors to identify and select people on the basis of these. In this chapter we are going to focus on some of the easier steps that you can take as a leader to ensure your recruitment is strengths-focused.

Getting people talking about their strengths

In its simplest form, strengths-focused recruitment involves getting people to talk about and reveal their strengths during the recruitment process. In strengths-focused recruitment there is a shift away from a focus on *'What can you do?'* (typically, this might involve assessing people against competencies) towards *'What do you enjoy or love doing and, therefore, what do you do well?'* As a result, there is more opportunity to learn about the real person and select the individual who is the best fit for the job.

There are several things you will notice when people talk about their strengths. You will see and sense the energy and enthusiasm that comes from people when they talk about what they love doing and what energises them. This sort of genuine energy cannot be faked. You will see it in their animated body language, and hear it in the tone, pitch and pace of their voice, and the words they use. You will hear words such as 'really enjoy', 'love', etc.

Focusing on strengths, not competencies

Used to its full potential, strengths-focused recruitment moves away from traditional competency-based selection. Instead it uses a process that identifies the strengths required within a role and selects people not just on the basis of whether they will perform well in aspects of the role, but also whether they will derive energy and fulfilment when carrying out the role.

Some organisations have taken the step of identifying core strengths required for a role, similar to the way an organisation might identify competencies, and then build their selection process around this. Assessment centres can also be designed to enable people to demonstrate their strengths as they take part in work-based scenarios and allow the observers to spot the high performance and high energy that comes from people using their strengths.

Strengths-focused interviews

Organisations dipping their toe in the 'strengths' water can strengthen their recruitment process by designing strengths-focused interviews. Strengths-focused interviews that encourage candidates to talk about their strengths create a more positive and engaging experience for the candidates, allowing them to more easily reveal their innate attributes and articulate what it is that energises them and drives their best performance at work.

Identifying people's strengths during the interview provides very useful information to feed into the recruitment decision and determine whether someone is a good fit for the job based not just on their experience and competence, but, equally importantly, on their strengths.

How do I conduct a strengths-focused interview?

We offer below some strengths-focused questions that you can use to create a strengths-focused interview. The sets of questions are available for downloading at our website www.sfleadership.co.uk, so that you can create your own interview structure. You can select the questions you think will work best for your selection needs, and you can of course design some strengths-focused questions of your own.

Setting the scene

When you adopt a strengths approach in your recruitment, candidates will always notice a difference; it won't feel like the interviews that they have experienced in the past. In order to prepare them for something that will feel a bit different, it is a good idea for the interviewer to explain the approach that they will take. For example:

▌ We are particularly keen to find out about you as a person, your strengths and attributes, as well as what you are interested in. So, as well as exploring your experience and your skills, we will also be asking you questions about what you find most energising or when you find that you are at your best.

You might also want to start the interview off on a positive note by asking them a question like:

▌ Tell me about a successful and energising day that you have had recently.

Or

▌ Tell me about something that you have done recently that you were really proud of.

And then follow up with questions such as:

▌ What did you find especially energising and enjoyable about it?

▌ What did that experience tell you about the sort of things you are really good at and enjoy doing at work?

Exploring strengths

If you would like to generate a clear idea of the candidate's strengths – what they believe they are good at and what energises them – there are a number of very powerful questions you can ask:

▌ Tell me about a work situation where you were doing something that you really enjoyed and were getting good results in?

▌ What did you enjoy about it?

▌ When do you feel like you are most like yourself at work?

▌ When are you at your best?

▌ What do you love doing?

▌ What energises you?

▌ What comes easily to you?

▌ What sort of things do you tend to learn most quickly?

▌ When do you find that you get most engaged and energised in your work?

For a potential job to be a good 'fit' for someone there must be opportunities within it for the individual to play to their strengths. You can ask:

▌ From what you have said you have highlighted that you have strengths in . . ., is that right? What opportunities do you see to play to your strengths and use them more within the role you are applying for?

▌ What could you do to ensure that you have the opportunity to play to these strengths within the role you are applying for?

Identifying untapped potential

We all have strengths that we do not get enough opportunity to use. Changing job roles is an ideal opportunity for individuals to consider what these untapped strengths might be and to choose a role, or even shape a role, that will provide opportunities to put these strengths to work, thus leading to higher levels of performance, engagement and job satisfaction.

During the interview process, you help people reveal some of these hidden strengths by asking questions such as:

▌ What do you love doing at work, and believe you do well, but don't get the opportunity to do very often at the moment?

▌ What do you really love doing at work that you wish you could do more often?

▌ What opportunities do you perceive within the role you are applying for that will allow you to use these strengths/do these things more?

Discovering learned behaviours

In work we strive to be good at what we have to do and we often believe that we need to be exceptional in every aspect of our job role or the organisation's competency framework. Many of these requirements of the job we find we can do to a very high standard, but we also find that they drain our energy. Being able to do something well, but also finding that we dread the thought of doing it, is a sure sign of a 'learned behaviour'. Learned behaviours do not lead to individuals giving of their best and are therefore something to be aware of when selecting the right person for a role.

To identify learned behaviours, you can ask questions such as:

▌ What sort of things do people tell you that you are good at, that you actually find draining?

▌ What sort of things do you always leave until last? What sort of things are always left on your 'to do' list, or left unfinished?

▌ What aspects of your work do you do well, but don't find very interesting or engaging? What do you do to get around this?

Linking them to the job being applied for, you could ask:

▌ To what extent do you foresee the need to do such tasks in the role you are applying for?

▌ How could you manage this so that you maintain your effectiveness and your fulfilment at work?

Discussing weaknesses

This is always a tricky area in the selection process, since it is questionable how honest people will be about their weaknesses when they really want the job! You could introduce this by saying something like:

▌ We are not all good at everything, and we don't expect people to be. We notice that the things that we are not good at often de-energise us . . .

You can then ask:

▌ What do you perform less well in that also de-energises you?

▌ What have you done in the past to compensate for these aspects?

▌ How important do you believe these aspects will be in your new role?

▌ If important, what could you do to develop these aspects, or call on other strengths that you have to help you?

Linking strengths to competencies

It is very likely that you will want to talk to people about their skills and experience, and you may be required to assess their level of capability against critical aspects of the role, or against a set of competencies.

A strengths focus can also be added to traditional competency-based interview questions, by asking further questions about the individual's reaction to the task or situation. For example, when a candidate describes their response to a question such as: 'Can you tell me about a time when you have successfully coordinated a team of people towards achieving a challenging goal', you can ask further follow-on questions, such as:

▌ What did you particularly enjoy about that situation?

▌ How did you feel about this situation you found yourself in?

▌ Was there anything you didn't enjoy about it?

People's responses will help you identify whether the activities described were enjoyable and energising to them. They might give responses that indicate they were loving the challenge of the task, feeling highly energised and getting great results. This is a sure sign of a strength that can be re-applied in a future role.

In the real world . . .

Here is an example of an organisation incorporating a strengths focus into their recruitment process.

One of my (Kathy's) clients was restructuring their organisation and was carrying out a series of internal selection interviews for new roles. This organisation was keen to take the opportunity that the restructure offered to introduce a strengths approach to their interviews. They used many of the questions offered in this chapter to give their interviews a definite strengths flavour. Both the interviewers and the interviewees noticed the difference straight away. They were pleased to notice how much more lively, animated and positive the interview experience was for both parties. The interviewers told us that it was much easier to see the real person when they got them talking about their strengths, and hence it made the selections much more effective. Candidates also felt that they had given their best and shown their best self, whether or not they got offered the position.

How do I prepare to recruit with a strengths focus?

Become skilled at 'strengths-spotting'

If you are involved in the selection process you will want to ensure you are really good at 'strengths spotting', as if you are looking at people through 'strengths-tinted lenses'[1] so that you can pay full attention to the signs of people's strengths.

When you are interviewing, you will not necessarily have the opportunity to see strengths in action, so you need to make sure you are able to recognise the signs of someone talking about a strength. Bear in mind, too, that the animation that people show when they talk about their strengths can sometimes be displayed more subtly with those who are more introvert in nature. If you have the opportunity to observe people in selection activities as part of an assessment centre, then you have more of an opportunity to spot those strengths.

Write your interview questions and practise

When you have devised your interview questions and recruitment 'script', maybe using the questions we offered above, it is a good idea to run some practice sessions. This is not just so that you can practise using your strengths-focused questions, but also so that you can experience the positive and energising effect of being interviewed in this way. These practice sessions will also allow you to take on board any suggestions to improve your questions and process.

If you have a team of people involved in the recruitment process, you may find it useful to introduce the recruitment team to the strengths approach first (see Chapter 6 for ideas about how you can do this).

Be consistent

If you profess to adopt a strengths focus and tell your candidates that you are using a strengths approach in your recruitment because of its fit with your overall culture, you will want to make sure that all other interactions that the candidate has with your team and the organisation give them a similar sense of the strengths-focused philosophy at work throughout the organisation. For example, you will want to make sure

---

[1] Linley, A. (2008) *Average to A+: Realising strengths in yourself and others*, Coventry, CAPP Press.

that your offer letter and induction process have a strengths flavour, or that your early team meetings adopt a strengths focus, etc. On our website www.sfleadership.com, we have a free additional chapter that you can download, which will give you some very useful information about strengths-focused induction and how to do it.

What are my next steps?

If you want to 'strengthen' your recruitment process, here are some steps to help you implement it:

1. Make sure your recruitment process fits with your overall company culture and philosophy. If you have a strengths focus at the heart of your organisation's philosophy you already have a head start, and it makes sense to send out this message clearly right from the start of the recruitment process.

2. Decide how your recruitment advertising will communicate your focus on strengths. For example, 'We are looking for people who love doing . . . and are energised by . . .'. This is an opportunity for you to 'strengthen' your brand and reputation when people sense the energy of the organisation.

3. Decide how you want to introduce strengths into your recruitment process. Do you want to start by ensuring that your one-to-one interviews are strengths-focused? Do you wish to identify a framework of strengths (core strengths and those related to individual roles)? Do you want to add a strengths focus to the whole selection process, including assessment centres?

4. Re-design the selection process, or create a task team, or bring in external expertise to help you with this. Keeping it simple, you can use some of the questions we provide to add a strengths emphasis to your existing interview material and decide how you want to record the strengths you identify.

5. Communicate with those involved in the selection process and ensure that they are adept at 'strengths spotting', have a strengths-focused mindset and are practised in the new approach. (See Chapter 6 for introducing a strengths approach to others.)

6. Determine how you will brief candidates about what to expect at their forthcoming interview.

7 Decide how you will offer feedback. Offering strengths-focused feedback can enhance the selection process for all candidates, even unsuccessful ones.

8 Enjoy the experience and notice the results!

Strengths-focused recruitment

1 Take a look at your existing recruitment processes. How strengths-focused are they?

2 Determine what you need to do to introduce more of a strengths approach to your recruitment processes. Is this something you can do on your own, or do you need to enlist the help of your Human Resources team?

3 Download the templates on our website for some useful strengths-focused questions that you can use in the interview.

4 Liaise with your Human Resources team or those responsible for the organisation's recruitment processes and let them know what changes you would like to make.

5 Practise having some strengths-focused interviews and notice the results.

part

Applying a strengths focus to business challenges

Part 2 of this book first focused on how to identify and develop your own strengths and those of your team. It then explained how to apply a strengths-focused mindset to your day-to-day interactions with your team, in ad hoc conversations as well as regular meetings or structured coaching sessions. Finally it outlined ways to develop employee processes (performance appraisal, development planning and recruitment) that your team or organisation can use to support and develop a strengths-focused culture.

There are other broader, longer-term and more strategic considerations for a leader. We address three important aspects of these in the third and final part of the book:

1 How can I create a high-performing team that is strength focused? (Chapter 15)

2 How can I lead others through change in a strengths-focused way? (Chapter 16)

3 How can I create and implement strategy with a strengths-focused approach? (Chapter 17)

These chapters can be read independently of the rest of the book. As we have done generally throughout the book, we will also highlight which chapters expand on the areas mentioned, should you wish to explore any particular point in more depth.

15 Building high-performing teams

The way a team plays as a whole determines its success. You may have the greatest bunch of individual stars in the world, but if they don't play together, the club won't be worth a dime.
(Babe Ruth, baseball legend)

IF YOU'VE HAD AN OPPORTUNITY to implement any of the four steps of our MORE model, you will already be doing activities that help create a high-performing team focused on strengths. This chapter looks to add to all of those useful activities by highlighting the key 'how to' of high-performing teams.

Many of our clients choose to introduce strengths to their team to increase the collective team performance. Much of our work is about enabling teams to become high-performing teams. What we aim to do in this chapter is share with you some of the approaches we use. This will give you some practical ideas and approaches to build the performance of your own team.

By the end of this chapter you will have answers to the following questions:

1. What is a high-performing team and how does a focus on strengths help to create one?
2. What impact does a leader have on the level of team performance?
3. What are the six steps that create a high-performing team?
4. How are my team performing against these six steps?

What is a high-performing team and how does a focus on strengths help to create one?

Teams come in all shapes and sizes. You will probably have been a member of many teams in your life so far, some at work and some outside of work, such as sports teams, choirs, music bands, quiz teams and some types of clubs.

So what is it that makes a group of people a team? We like the following definition:[1]

> A small number of people with complementary skills who are committed to a common purpose, set of performance goals, and shared approach for which they hold themselves mutually accountable.

The 'shared approach' needs to include:[2]

▌ ways of effectively meeting and communicating that raise morale and alignment;

▌ ways of effectively engaging with all the team's key stakeholder groups;

▌ ways that individuals and the team can continually learn and develop.

The small number of people mentioned above is ideally 10 or less. Teams larger than that generally have significant challenges in working effectively as one team.

Workgroup or real team?

Low   High
interdependence   interdependence

Work group   Real team

One other important point to consider about your own team is the level of interdependence needed in the team in order for it to achieve its goals. A

---

[1] Katzenbach, J. R. and Smith, D.K. (1993) *The Wisdom of Teams: Creating the high-performance organization*, Boston, MA, Harvard Business School Press.

[2] Hawkins, P. (2011) *Leadership Team Coaching: Developing collective transformational leadership*, London, Kogan Page.

cricket or baseball team doesn't have the same level of interdependence that a football or rugby team does. In baseball and cricket, for the team that is batting, we get the team score simply by adding up the scores of individual performers. In rugby and football, we need the team to play and closely interact with one another in order to score goals and points. These teams have a high level of interdependence.

So think of your own team. How much is it a cricket or baseball team, and how much a rugby or football team? The more it needs to be a football or rugby team, the more you will want to develop the effectiveness of the team. The more it needs to be a cricket or baseball team, the less useful devoting time to increasing team interaction and team-building activities will be. How much interdependence is desirable in your team in order for it to be high-performing?

Before answering that question it may be useful for you to be clear about what we mean by high-performing. When working with teams we often ask them about their experiences of being in high-performing teams. What is it that characterises a high-performing team? Time and time again the following characteristics appear in their descriptions, and these are backed up by studies of high-performing teams.

Characteristics of a high-performing team:

▌ meets the definition of a team (above);

▌ deep commitment to one another's personal growth and success;

▌ exceptional performance – outperform all reasonable expectations of the group, including those of the team members themselves;

▌ high levels of enthusiasm and energy;

▌ great stories of 'galvanising events' – turning points in their history where they overcame the odds.[3]

A number of writers on teams have created models to understand these aspects of high-performing teams by simplifying the detailed descriptions

---

[3] Adapted from Katzenbach, J. R. and Smith, D. K. (1993) *The Wisdom of Teams: Creating the high-performance organization*, Boston, MA, Harvard Business School Press.

into a small number of key elements.[4] If we look at what they have in common you'll see that they generally highlight three elements of high-performing teams:

Three elements of a high-performing team:

1 **Task.** The team delivers products or services which meet or exceed expected standards of its stakeholders.

2 **Team-working.** The team continually enhances its ability to work as a team (both within the team itself and with others outside the team) and so improves its ability to deliver on its task.

3 **Individual.** Individual team members experience well-being, fulfilment and development, in relation to their work in the team.

Put simply you could say that members of a high-performing team work very well with one another and with others outside the team, they deliver high performance, and at the same time each individual enjoys their own role in the team.

The evidence around high-performing teams

The Gallup organisation have done a huge amount of work investigating the relationship between strengths and individual, team and organisational success. They interviewed over one million employees and 20,000 leaders across the world in a variety of sectors. From this research they came up with a number of findings, two of which are particularly relevant to leaders of teams and organisations.[5]

First they found that in organisations where leaders fail to focus on employees' strengths the odds of an employee being engaged were 1 in 11 (9 per cent). In organisations where leaders do focus on their employees'

---

4   Some of these are: Hackman, J. R. (1987) 'The Design of Work Teams', in J. Lorsch (ed.), *Handbook of Organizational Behaviour*, New York, Prentice-Hall, pp. 315–42. Sundstrom, E., De Meuse, K. and Futtrell, D. (1990) 'Work Teams: Applications and effectiveness', *American Psychologist* 45 (2), pp. 120–33. Adair, J. (1987) *Effective Team Building*, London, Pan Books. Katzenbach, J. R. and Smith, D. K. (1993). *The Wisdom of Teams: Creating the high-performance organization*, Boston, MA, Harvard Business School Press. Hackman, J. R. (2002). *Leading Teams: Setting the stage for great performances*, Boston, MA, Harvard Business School Press. Drexler, A. B., Sibbet, D. and Forrester, R. H (1988) 'The Team Performance Model', in W. B. Reddy and K. Jamison (eds.) *Team Building: Blueprints for Productivity and Satisfaction*, Alexandria, Virginia and San Diego: NTL Institute for Applied Behavioral Science and University Associates, Inc., pp. 45–62.

5   Rath, T. and Conchie, B. (2008). *Strengths Based Leadership: Great leaders, teams, and why people follow*, New York, Gallup Press.

strengths the chance of employees being engaged went up to 3 in 4 (75 per cent). These higher engagement levels also translate into stronger productivity and bottom-line results, as well as higher levels of well-being for each employee. They also identified that it is the individual's local manager who has most influence on that engagement, with organisational leadership being a smaller though still relevant factor.

So in a well-rounded team we will find team members who know one another's strengths and then assign roles or tasks according to individual strengths (rather than rigidly following job roles).

How high-performing teams communicate

The research around the nature of communication in high-performing teams has some strong links to a strengths focus. We mentioned the two researchers[6] who found that in high-performing teams there was a ratio of appreciation to criticism of 6:1; in medium-performing teams it was 2:1 or lower; and in low-performing teams it was well below 1:1. This echoes much of the emphasis in this book on the value of focusing on our strengths (and those of others in our team) and what we are doing well. Our guess is that we have a virtuous circle here – the better we do the easier it becomes to be appreciative, and the more noticing and appreciative we are about what is working well, the easier it is to do more of it. I have no doubt that this is the kind of team you want to be leading, if you are not already doing so.

What impact does a leader have on the level of team performance?

So, in looking at the evidence around the value of a strengths focus in teams the last area we will look at connects two separate but related research topics: first, the impact that effective leaders have on teams, and secondly, the value of a strengths focus in increasing your effectiveness as a leader.

We are sure that somewhere along the line you will have experienced the positive benefits of working in a team with an effective leader.

---

[6] Losada, M. and Heaphy, E. (2004) 'The Role of Positivity and Connectivity in the Performance of Business Teams: A nonlinear dynamics model', *American Behavioral Scientist* 47, pp. 740–65.

Recent research[7] by Zenger, Folkman and their colleagues has been able to define some of the key impacts of an effective leader. In the research stakeholders rated a leader's effectiveness and the data was then correlated with a variety of aspects of high performance in teams and organisations. The most effective leaders, as judged by their 360 degree feedback, achieve much higher sales figures and better customer satisfaction. They also achieve higher staff satisfaction, engagement, commitment and retention.

It was these same researchers who found that leaders whose development plans focused on building their strengths got three times greater improvement in their 360 degree feedback ratings than did those who focused on fixing their weaknesses. Their overall 360 degree feedback ratings were also considerably higher than the weakness-focused leaders, 77 per cent effective compared to 46 per cent.

So you have a hugely significant role in the success of your team, and you will enhance that powerful influence by building your strengths.

What are the six steps that create a high-performing team?

Many writers on teams and leading teams have put forward a variety of models to describe the sequence of steps a leader can take to go about building a high performing team[8]. These models have many elements in common, but 'cut the cake' in slightly different ways. They are listed in our footnote if you would like to explore them further.

We've worked with teams in a variety of organisations across a number of sectors. We've trained leaders in building high-performing teams. To support this work, we have developed our own six-step model as a very useful framework for understanding how to build a great team.

---

[7] See Zenger, J. H., et al. (2012) *How to Be Exceptional: Drive leadership success by magnifying your strengths*, New York, McGraw-Hill. They show the link between leadership effectiveness and business success, and also the link between greater perceived leadership effectiveness via 360 degree feedback scores and the focus on developing strengths as opposed to weaknesses.

[8] Hawkins, P. (2011) *Leadership Team Coaching: Developing collective transformational leadership*, London, Kogan Page. Schwartz, R. M. (2013) *Smart Leaders, Smart Teams: How you and your team get unstuck to get results*, San Francisco, Jossey-Bass. Adair, J. (1987) *Effective Team Building*, London, Pan Books. Katzenbach, J. R. and Smith, D.K. (1993) *The Wisdom of Teams: Creating the high-performance organization*, Boston, Mass., Harvard Business School Press. Hackman, J. R. (2002) *Leading Teams: Setting the stage for great performances*, Boston, Mass., Harvard Business School Press.

We will explain the six steps to a high-performing team below, and offer it to you as a way to assess how well your own team has covered each of them. As we go through the six steps we'll highlight the points at which the strengths focus plays a particularly significant role.

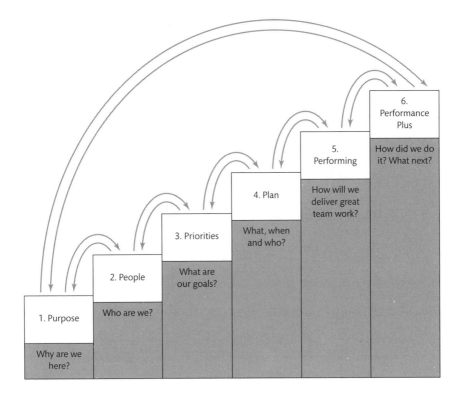

The model outlines that, in building a high-performing team, the process broadly follows these six steps, particularly for a brand new team, or one which has seen significant changes in its purpose. Of course there may be some changes in team membership, stakeholder expectations, or other variables which may change the nature of the team – hence the backwards and forwards arrows.

Here are each of the steps:

Step	Activity	Strengths focus
1. Purpose Why are we here?	A feature of high-performing teams is that team members are very clear and very committed to the aim or purpose of the team. Time and energy should be put into getting to this point early on in the life of a team. It should be revisited regularly.	Our purpose will ideally be something that allows us to play to our strengths. Our strengths should suit our purpose.
2. People Who are we?	For people to work well together, it is important that they know one another's strengths, values and motivations. Teams should make time to do this exploration.	Identifying one another's strengths (and weaknesses) is an important part of knowing who is in the team and what they bring to the table. (Chapters 6, 7, and 8 show you how to do this.) It's also useful for the team to have an overview of its collective strengths, and significant weaknesses, by pooling the individual data.
3. Priorities What are our goals?	To deliver on the purpose of the team, the team needs to clarify what success with the team purpose will look like at some point in the future. What are the deliverables? How will we measure our success? It will also be useful for the team to know what individual goals people have, and what they want to get from their membership of the team.	The goals should take account of the team's strengths (and weaknesses).

4. Plan What, when and who?	At this stage the individual strengths that team members bring can be aligned with the roles they will take in achieving the team's goals. A clear plan of action to achieve the team's goals is created. Each individual knows what he or she needs to contribute in order for the team to succeed. Team members can share their expectations of one another.	The team spends time ensuring that individual strengths and roles are matched in a way that plays to the team's strengths. The action plan for each individual will ideally play to his or her strengths. Based on the team's knowledge of individual strengths, complimentary role sharing can be planned where useful.
5. Performing How will we deliver great teamwork?	The team clarifies what processes, systems and behaviours it needs to have in place in the team for the team to succeed. This will include communication, information sharing, decision making, conflict management, etc. How the team will work effectively with stakeholders will also be considered.	Communication processes, e.g. team meetings, and one-to-one reviews, will want to ensure they focus on building individual and team strengths, as opposed to a focus on problems/weakness. See Chapters 9–13 for a variety of ways to build these strengths-focused processes.
6. Performance Plus – How did we do it? What do we do next?	The team will have a process in place to regularly review its achievements, celebrate and reflect on how its success was achieved, and what to learn from it in terms of planning the next steps. It will also address any critical weaknesses or failings, and what to learn from them to create greater success.	The process will ensure that there is a focus on strengths and achievement in order to build and enhance the team's success. This will obviously be balanced with the need to take on any learning from critical weaknesses or failings. Weakness will be managed from a position of strength. See Chapters 9–13 for a variety of ways to continually focus on strengths.

How are my team performing against these six steps?

It is useful for a team to step back from the day-to-day and ask, 'How well are we performing as a team?' The six steps listed provide a useful framework to do that assessment. A team leader can invite their team to score how well the team is achieving each of the steps. To support teams to look at their performance in more detail, we have developed a questionnaire which breaks these seven steps down into finer detail. For more information on the Six Steps Team Effectiveness Assessment, visit our website www.sfleadership.co.uk.

Your own assessment

Getting feedback from your team in this way allows you to gain some clarity about where you are currently doing well as a team leader, and where your next steps may be in developing your team. It also allows the team itself to openly measure and develop its effectiveness.

The assessment of your stakeholders

Effective teams are also outward-looking as well as inward-looking. So as well as their own view of their effectiveness, they will recognise the value of having feedback from stakeholders. The key stakeholders may be some/all of the following:

▌ staff from other teams who report into this team;

▌ other parts of the organisation that regularly interface with the team;

▌ those the team report to;

▌ customers (internal and external);

▌ partners, suppliers and other external bodies;

▌ investors and regulators.

A team 360 degree metric could be carefully tailored for your own particular team. However, a simple self-administered measurement could be done by any team keen to learn how to enhance its performance further. Simple strengths-focused questions could be:

1. How would you rate this team's delivery: 1–10?

2. What do you most appreciate and value about what you receive from this team?

3   If this team's performance was (even) better for you, what would be different?

4   What do you most appreciate and value about how this team engages with you?

5   If this team's working relationship with you was (even) better, what would be different?

Taking action

These assessments then provide a useful starting point to plan a team development programme that will focus on developing the team from Step 1 through to Step 6, or those steps which could most benefit the team. Getting the lower steps right will tend to make any of the higher steps easier to achieve.

Here is a real example of this kind of work:

In the real world . . .

Jerry Clough, a managing director in an organisation within the NHS, describes the work we did with his team:

A strengths-based approach seemed to fit really well with what I was looking for – a new organisation, looking to take on the best of what had gone before whilst taking on the expectation of radical change and, critically, with a group of staff who had gone through over 18 months of uncertainty and a difficult environment. We tried a few introductory sessions on strengths-based leadership to test the approach and there was a really good natural view of this being a 'right thing to do'.

We then embedded strengths in to all of our development activity. Online individual (with 360 degree feedback) and team assessments were key to that, but almost more important was how we used strengths to change the language of how we described organisations, ourselves as a team and each of us individually. It took a while for the team to accept that basing sessions on things that had gone well and where we could talk about the strengths we brought to those projects or issues was a good use of time. But we soon found it much easier to then focus on how we were going to improve the performance of the team and organisation and address the many challenges that were around us. Members of the leadership team had strengths-based 1:1 coaching and this really helped to amplify the group-based learning.

There were two main questions: does this apparently happy-clappy approach actually work? and what about focusing on the real issues, rather than just the nice things that have gone well? The team is in a very different place now and, as one of four key units in the organisation, has led the way that others are now keen to follow because they have seen the results. The team is close and well connected and able to see what each of their colleagues brings to any situation. Others see this and are taken by the positive, can-do attitude of mutual respect that is engendered. And we tackle the really big issues – this definitely isn't about pretending that our issues aren't the huge challenge that they are every day. It is, though, about taking them on with the right attitude, trust in your team and with a real sense of finding the best skills we have to address the particular dilemma.

We have now refined our recruitment and performance appraisal processes to be more strengths-focused and have seen extremely positive improvements compared to what we had before.

And looking back: how did we doubt that this made sense? Why would I want to spend all my life inflating my weaknesses through continued focus and attention? I like working with my team. They can describe what they do really well and who would be best in the team for the particular task ahead.

Jerry Clough

Chief Operating Officer

Northern, Eastern and Western Devon Clinical Commissioning Group

An example of a strengths-focused team development plan is shown in Appendix 3.

ACTION POINTS

Building high-performing teams

1. If they would be happy to do so, involve your team members in assessing how well the team has done each of the six steps.
2. For a more detailed assessment of the effectiveness of your team, visit our website at www.sfleadership.co.uk.
3. Involve your stakeholders in giving you 'team' feedback so that you have a more balanced external and internal view of your team's effectiveness.
4. To build higher performance in the team focus on each step sequentially, using our suggested activities.
5. Use all the suggestions of the book so far to 'strengthen' your team.

Leading change

People don't resist change. They resist being changed.
(Peter Senge, author and director of the Center for Organizational
Learning at the MIT Sloan School of Management)

AS A LEADER or perhaps as an employee you may have had a variety of
experiences of change. Some of that may be positive, but, more likely,
some not so positive. I take that slightly negative position because of the
research on change within organisations. It presents a somewhat sobering
fact: in 1995 only 30 per cent of change programmes in organisations
were succeeding.[1] In 2006 the figure had not changed![2]

So what is it that the 30 per cent do? And how does the answer to that
question relate to our focus on strengths? What does this mean for you
when you are a strengths-focused leader?

By the end of this chapter you will have answers to the following
questions:

1. What are the benefits of a strengths-focused approach to introducing
   and implementing change?

2. How do I manage change in a strengths-focused way?

---

[1] Kotter, J. P. (1995) 'Leading Change: Why transformation efforts fail', *Harvard Business Review*,
    March–April 1995, p. 1.

[2] Isern, J. and Pung, C. (2006) 'Organizing for Successful Change Management: A McKinsey global
    survey', *The McKinsey Quarterly*, June 2006.

What are the benefits of a strengths-focused approach to introducing and implementing change?

To get some evidence about successful change programmes we can go to the global consultancy McKinsey[3] who survey large organisations around the world. A survey they conducted in 2010 asked executives about their organisation's experience of change programmes. They were able to identify a few tactics that were common to successful transformational change programmes. These tactics included:

▌ setting clear, aspirational targets;

▌ creating a clear structure for how the change process will work;

▌ maintaining energy, involvement and collaboration throughout the whole organisation as early as possible in the process;

▌ exercising strong leadership;

▌ focusing on strengths and achievements, not just problems, throughout the entire transformation process.

You'll see that the last point on the list of tactics above mentions a focus on strengths and achievements, not just problems. McKinsey's survey found that the more change programmes focused solely on fixing problems the less successful they were. A focus on strengths and achievements, and not just problems, throughout the entire transformation process was strongly tied to success.

You will notice how this echoes the same principles that we have highlighted throughout this book, and supports the evidence we have presented around a strengths-focused approach to building individual and team performance.

How do I manage change in a strengths-focused way?

So the evidence shows that approaching change with a 'deficit' or 'weakness' mindset is not effective. Focusing solely on fixing what's

---

[3]   McKinsey and Company (2010) *What Successful Transformations Share: McKinsey Global Survey results.* www.mckinsey.com/insights/organization/what_successful_transformations_share_mckinsey_global_survey_results. Accessed 21.7.14.

wrong tends to drain energy, reinforce a negative team/organisation identity, foster lower morale, restrict creativity and innovation, and weaken teamwork and relationships. It will also tend to restrict the focus to the past rather than create vivid and positive images of the future.

So what does a strengths-focused approach to leading change look like? Using the principles of successful change outlined above, here is a four-stage approach to strengths-focused change:

1   preparing yourself and your mindset;

2   launching a change project;

3   progress reviews;

4   ending a change project.

Preparing yourself and your mindset

Earlier in the book we saw that the field of psychology tells us that our behaviour is driven by our mindset and emotions and that these shape our behaviour, which determines our results. So it is obviously important for a leader to approach a change programme with a positive mindset. A leader's mindset will affect the mindset of the team and the team's results. So here are our thoughts on a useful mindset for you to have when approaching change:

The mindset of a strengths-focused change leader

Better out than in! It is useful to acknowledge our feelings about the challenges we face. If these are not expressed constructively then they can create problems for us. As a leader how am I feeling about this change? Have I had the right opportunity to acknowledge or express my own feelings, so that I can then move on? I need to do it for myself before I can help my team do it.

Choose your attitude. Once you've acknowledged how you currently feel, explore what opportunities there are in the situation, as well as the challenges, and choose the attitude to it that will empower you and your team most. You cannot control events, but you can control your attitude and response to them.

What we focus on grows. If we focus on the way we want things to be we are more likely to achieve it. If we stay focused on what we or others are doing wrong we are likely to get stuck there. Solution talk creates solutions and problem talk creates problems.

▌ People increase their confidence for change when they build on what they know works. If we highlight what has worked for us in previous change efforts, or other challenges, we build confidence to do it again.

▌ The process of asking questions influences those answering them. The type of question we ask actually affects the thinking and feeling and therefore the energy of those we are asking. Asking staff, 'Where are we failing? What are we doing wrong? Whose fault is this? How can we minimise the negative effects?' will have a very different impact to asking 'How have we successfully managed change before now? How will we benefit from managing it successfully now?' Choose your questions wisely.

Launching a change project

So as a leader, early in a change project, you will want to help your staff and stakeholders by communicating the following:

▌ **Clarify the facts (WHAT).** What will be changing and what won't?

▌ **Clarify the positive purpose of the change project (WHY).** Explain the business, political or organisational reasons for the change. Why does the change have to happen?

▌ **Explain and discuss the challenges.** Explain what some of the challenges may be, and for whom. Involve people in sharing their ideas on this.

▌ **Explain what success looks like.** Explain the time frame for the change and the positive outcomes that will be there when the change is implemented.

▌ **Explain what's in it for each stakeholder.** Explain what will be the benefit to each individual in the new world. Cover all of the following:

  – Customers

  – The team

  – The organisation

  – Other key stakeholders

  – Society in general

  – Each individual staff member.

Again, involve people in contributing their own ideas on these points. Research shows[4] that the clearer you are about how all of these stakeholders will benefit, the more positively employees will engage with the change. If you only mention or discuss the benefit to customers (who are only one of your stakeholders), this is not as powerful an argument for change.

▋ **Make communication two-way.** It's already been alluded to, but it is so important it is worth mentioning separately. Explain that there will be an opportunity for them to discuss and share their ideas and feelings about the change and the way forward, as well as give their own suggestions and ideas.

▋ **Allow people the space to voice concerns or anxieties.** If you don't, they will come out anyway, often in less constructive ways, and in ways that limit the progress of the change project.

▋ **Acknowledge the potential difficulties and challenges.** People are more likely to engage with you if they can see that you understand their perspective and concerns.

▋ **Identify the relevant individual and collective successes and strengths we bring to a change project from previous experiences.** From as early as possible and throughout the project, refer to the achievements, successes, and strengths of the team or group. Doing this genuinely will create an ongoing resource of energy.

▋ **Build a detailed and compelling picture of what a successful change project will deliver in terms of results and people's experience of it.** As far as possible, involve everyone in doing this with you. There may be some aspects of the change project that are 'givens', but people can still be involved in deciding how they will best achieve these.

▋ **Identify the strengths we will need in order to succeed.** Who has them? Do we have them all? How do we cover for those we don't have? If people can contribute from their own strengths, they will do so with more engagement and with more competence and confidence. Use complementary role sharing to engage people.

▋ **Communicate often and in a variety of ways (and in ways that focus on strengths).** Keep people abreast of what's happening regularly and in a variety of ways that suit the different communication preferences. In any communication acknowledge the challenges, and highlight the strengths and capabilities on show in the group.

---

[4] Keller, S. and Price, C. (2011) *Beyond Performance: How great organizations build ultimate competitive advantage*, Hoboken, NJ, Wiley.

▌**Be a role model.** You will be communicating your mindset with your words and deeds. People will look to you for cues, right down to your enthusiasm, energy, and body language, so don't forget this aspect of communicating and managing the change process. As Gandhi said, 'Be the change you want to see in the world.' People will follow your example.

▌**Create a clear structure and plan for the change.** Involve people in creating a clear plan for implementing the change successfully. The evidence shows this is a key element of successful change initiatives.

Progress reviews

As you make the journey through the period of change you will want to review progress in a way that asks:

▌**Our successes so far: how have we done it and what has been the positive impact?** Start every review meeting with these questions. This will create the optimism and the energy to take on the next steps, and the challenges that may be ahead. It will obviously identify strengths on show. If people have been having a tough time, it may be necessary to first of all let them voice these challenges, before then asking them about their successes.

▌**How well are we doing against our goals?** Where are we doing best? Where can we improve? Having a clear idea of progress made helps people to be more specific about what to do next and how to transfer the success from one area to another.

▌**What are the useful lessons from what we haven't achieved?** Come to your problems or weaknesses from a position of strength. By viewing problems, challenges and weaknesses as an opportunity to learn something useful for the way ahead, we avoid a restrictive and limiting blame culture. We can then build a picture of what we will be doing successfully, having learnt the useful lessons.

▌**What will further success look like?** What challenges will we want to overcome, and how will we do that? Have a detailed picture of not only the longer-term 'big' goal, but also a detailed, specific, measurable, motivating, achievable, time-framed description of the next steps ahead. This clarity sets people up for success.

Ending the change project

You will want to evaluate the project in a way which:

▌ Celebrates successes and how they were achieved. By learning what we did to create success, and by positively marking the achievement, we create motivation and confidence to take further steps. This creates the energy and results that characterise high-performing teams.

▌ Identifies key lessons which will be useful in the future. What else do we learn from our experience? What worked best in the process? What didn't work so well, and what is the useful lesson from that that we can put into practice next time?

Finally

Lastly, to lead change successfully you will want to attend to the two sides of strength: *competence* and *energy*. *Competence* is about getting the job done well, and *energy* is about people feeling inspired and motivated to do the job. Of course each one of these affects the other. In particular, inspiring people to want to positively engage with the change will create much stronger results. The quote below puts this more poetically:

> *If you want to build a ship, don't drum up people together to collect wood and don't assign them tasks and work, but rather teach them to long for the endless immensity of the sea.* (Antoine de Saint-Exupery, author)

ACTION POINTS

Leading change

1 Follow our suggestions for:

    i   preparing yourself and your mindset;

    ii launching a change project;

    iii progress reviews;

    iv ending a change project.

2 Build energy and involvement in the change by focusing on what's working and on strengths. Use that energy and involvement to tackle what could be working better, as well as any significant weaknesses.

17 Developing strategy

It is not in the stars to hold our destiny but in ourselves.
(William Shakespeare)

DOES THE WORD 'STRATEGY' EXCITE YOU, perhaps reminding you of many fruitful, creative and game-changing sessions you've had with your team or department? Or does it make you want to yawn and head for the first exit, so you can get on with something much more fun and purposeful?

Whatever your inclination, as a successful leader you will want to ensure that strategic thinking happens effectively in your team.

We have described the key elements of great leadership (in Chapter 4), drawn from recent research:

1. the ability to think strategically, to create a clear and compelling vision of the future;
2. the ability to communicate that vision in a way that inspires and motivates people to do what needs doing;
3. the ability to create engagement and strong relationships;
4. the ability to get things done;
5. the ability to change and improve, and to solve problems.

You may or may not have strategic mindedness as a strength yourself. Many successful leaders may not have. Gallup's research showed that while individual leaders are not well rounded, successful teams are. They have strengths in all the key areas. So if thinking strategically is not a strength of yours, we look at what you can do about that.

This chapter will not be an in-depth study of strategy. It will be more about showing how existing strategic processes can be more strengths-focused.

By the end of this chapter you will have answers to the following questions:

1 What's my approach to strategy?

2 What are the key elements of traditional strategic thinking?

3 How can I approach strategy with a strengths focus?

What's my approach to strategy?

According to your personality type you may either:

▌ enjoy focusing on what's right here, right now; enjoy a focus on detail, step-by-step specifics, practicalities, getting the tasks done;

OR

▌ enjoy thinking of what could be different in the future, how to change things for the better – the bigger-picture, broader-view of where to take things.

Thinking of our definition of a strength, strategy for you may be somewhere along the following spectrum:

I like doing it	I don't like doing it
It energises me	It drains me
I'm good at it	I'm not good at it

If it's a strength you'll probably enjoy reading the rest of the chapter, and seeing if it gives you further ideas on how you can build this strength of yours even further.

If this isn't a natural strength for you, you may want to think about how you can use your existing strengths to manage this weakness or non-strength. You may want to involve those who do have it as a strength to support and motivate you to do it. You may want to delegate elements of it to them. The rest of this chapter may give you other ideas of how you can ensure that strategy is done effectively in your team.

What are the key elements of traditional strategic thinking?

The clearer we are about the longer-term direction of our organisation, department or team over, say, the next three to five years, the clearer we will be about the outcomes we want to achieve over, say, the next six to 12 months. This longer-term view and the long-/medium-/short-term plans flowing from it are our strategy. Leaders have responsibility for creating strategy, and managers for implementing it. Put simply, the traditional elements of strategy are the answers to some very simple and important questions:

1 **Mission.** What's our purpose? What's our aim? What do we exist for?

2 **Vision.** Where do we want to get to (at some point in the future)?

3 **Values and behaviours.** What are the most important principles to focus on, so that we can deliver on our purpose and vision? What behaviours do we want to see, driven by these values/principles?

4 **Current position.** What are our current Strengths? What are our Weaknesses, Opportunities and Threats? (A traditional SWOT exercise.)

5 **Strategy.** What are the six to eight key areas for us to set goals in, in order to succeed? And what is the top-line outcome in each of these areas?

6 **Business plan.** How do we implement each strategic objective? Who will do what, in what time frame, with what resources?

How can I approach strategy with a strengths focus?

Your role in strengths-focused strategy is about leading the way in setting the longer-term direction for your team/department or organisation so that it can play to its strengths. In the last chapter, on leading change, we described how the strategy will get stronger results if everyone is engaged fully, and clear about the vision for the team.

So how do we create and implement strengths-focused strategy?

Well, it has much in common with the elements mentioned in the last chapter, but it does start with some more fundamental questions. We represent this below with the acronym **SPIRE**:

1. **S**trengths. What is that we are passionate about, can be best at, and can get great results at (our strengths)? This may take some thinking about, and plenty of discussion and listening to the perspective of each of our key stakeholder groups (customers, staff, shareholders, others).

2. **P**urpose. After considering our strengths, what is, or should be our aim/purpose as a team/department/organisation? Can we put it simply in a way we can all understand and engage with?

3. **I**mportant opportunities. What opportunities are there for us to build on those strengths and our purpose (internally and externally to our team/department/organisation)? If we have any important weaknesses, what useful lessons can we take from reflecting on those, which we can also use to our advantage? If we can see any threats on the horizon, either internally or externally, how can we respond to these in a way that will build on our strengths?

4. **R**ewarding future. After considering those opportunities, what or who do we want to be in the future? What will that look like for each of our key stakeholders? What will be important to us (our values)? What will be different about our behaviour? Involve people in discussing and answering these questions. Create a compelling and detailed picture of where we want to be.

5. **E**vidential results. Which key outcomes will evidence our success? Focus on a short list of key outcomes that are compelling, and that we are confident that we will achieve.

What follows these steps is the plan to deliver the compelling results. The business plan will ideally involve each individual in a team in an optimum way, by supporting them to play to their strengths within their role in implementing the strategy.

Strengths-focused strategy – how am I doing?

Check how well you are currently applying strengths-focused strategy, by doing a self-assessment on each of these questions.

Creating and implementing strengths-focused strategy	Scale 1–5 (1 = Not at all, 5 = Fully)				
	1	2	3	4	5
1. As a team/department/organisation we are all clear about what we are passionate about, can do best and can achieve great results in.					
2. The purpose or aim of my team/department/organisation is clear, motivating and understood by all my people and key stakeholders.					
3. My people and key stakeholders have been involved in creating a clear and compelling description of the future we want to create					
4. My people have clear expectations of the results we are aiming to achieve for each of our key stakeholders.					
5. There is a clear plan of action in my team as to how short-, medium- and long-term goals are to be achieved, and these play to the strengths of individuals in the team.					
6. My people are clear about how their day-to-day work connects to the vision of the team/department/organisation.					
7. Reports are given on the team's progress to the team and to relevant stakeholders.					
8. Stakeholders report positive outcomes and results.					
9. My people and key stakeholders have contributed to the creation of our strategy, and they have been involved in shaping its successful implementation.					
10. We celebrate our successes in achieving the strategic goals.					

This will have given you a clear idea of what you are currently doing well and where to build on it. There is huge value in asking your team and your stakeholders to rate the questions above from their perspective and involve them in identifying what needs to happen to score 5 on all 10 of the points. This could form an interesting first session when you are beginning to think about your team's strategic direction.

ACTION POINTS

Developing strategy

1 If developing strategy is your strength then play to it.

2 If developing strategy is not your strength, and is a significant weakness, use our suggestions (in Chapter 4) to manage it. This could be about tapping into your other strengths or the strengths of others that relate to strategy, eg Creativity, Analytical Thinking, Strategic Thinking, Planner, Common Sense, Detail Focus, etc.

3 Use the assessment to highlight areas for action.

4 Follow our SPIRE process to build strategy around strengths.

Putting it all together

We thought it would be useful for you to see the action points from the end of each chapter all in one place. You can use this to plan your own and your team's development over the medium to longer term. You can also download this from our website at www.sfleadership.co.uk

Chapter 2: The mindset of a strengths-focused leader

1. Do the five-day challenge and take the time to notice the impact of these strengths-focused habits.

2. Continue using the ones that are making a difference.

3. Notice the impact of these habits on your mindset as a leader.

4. Generally pay more attention to the way you talk about yourself and your team members. Raising your awareness of this will highlight your current mindset, affirm where it is already strong, and show you the opportunities to 'strengthen' it.

Chapter 3: Identifying my own strengths

1. Use one or more of our five methods to get very familiar with your strengths, untapped strengths, overplayed strengths, learned behaviours and weaknesses.

2. Look for opportunities to use your strengths more.

3. Consider how significant your weaknesses are to your performance.

4. Go on and work with our development tools (in Chapter 4). These will show you how to optimise your development.

Chapter 4: Developing my strengths and managing my weaknesses

1 Choose three to five strengths that you would like to develop and stand out for.

2 Create a strategy for developing these strengths and identify some actions you want to take (use the R5 Action Plan).

3 Notice the impact on your energy and performance as you work on developing these strengths.

4 Identify any significant weaknesses that need to be addressed.

5 Create a strategy for responding to the area(s) of weakness (use the R5 Action Plan).

6 Notice the impact on your performance as you work on improving the weakness.

Chapter 5: Aligning my goals and objectives with my strengths

1 If you already have business goals, go back and look at how you are playing to your strengths in the achievement of these goals. What more can you do to ensure that you are drawing on your strengths?

2 If you do not have business goals in place, use the template provided (Appendix 1) to design some SMARTIE goals that are aligned with your strengths.

3 If you already have some development goals, check how much these goals are focused on developing your strengths rather than your weaknesses. What can you do to make your development goals more focused on developing your strengths and only addressing significant weaknesses?

4 Use the template provided (Appendix 2) to design some new development goals that focus on developing your strengths and responding only to significant weaknesses.

Chapter 6: Introducing a strengths focus to others

1. Be clear about the reasons for introducing a strengths focus to your leadership and to your team. What results are you hoping for?

2. Decide on a method for introducing the concept of strengths to your team.

3. Be clear about what options are available to help your team identify their strengths. For example, will you coach people through completing their 5 Step Strengths Map (see Chapter 3) and R5 Action Plan (see Chapter 4)?

4. Prepare thoroughly for the 'Introducing a strengths focus' session with your team.

5. Think about the different possibilities for starting to introduce strengths to the team's way of working.

6. Allow your team to put forward their own ideas about how a strengths focus can be incorporated into the team's way of working.

7. Agree with the team some first steps for incorporating a strengths focus within the team.

Chapter 7: Identifying and developing strengths in others

1. Ensure that your team are open to exploring their strengths.

2. Ensure that there is a high level of trust and rapport between you and your team members. If not, think about what you need to do to build this trust.

3. Revisit what you know about a coaching approach – you will need to draw on these skills to explore people's strengths with them.

4. Decide on the approach you want to take to help your team members identify their strengths, using one of the methods described (in Chapter 3).

5. Set aside time to have conversations with each of your team members about how they can develop their strengths. Start by using the R5 Action Plan (see Chapter 4) and, if needed, explore some of the other options for developing strengths.

6. Remember to always take a coaching approach!

Chapter 8: Supporting others to manage their weaknesses

1   Take some time to consider each of your team members. In your view, what are their strengths and do they have any significant weaknesses? What is the impact of these significant weaknesses?

2   Consider how aware each team member is of any significant weaknesses. Depending on their current level of awareness, decide on the most appropriate way to discuss these weaknesses and create a plan to address them.

3   Work with each team member to create a plan to address any significant weaknesses.

4   Check in regularly with your direct report and offer feedback on progress and changes that you have observed.

Chapter 9: Day-to-day conversations

1   Strengthen your mindset by building the habit of:

    i   starting with an outcome focus;

    ii   focusing on what's working;

    iii managing weakness from strength.

2   If you think you are not already doing it, make a habit of focusing on what you want and what's working rather than what you don't want and what's not working.

3   To get the most from one-to-one conversations with your team members, use the six scripts until you can have these types of conversation without them. Download them from our website www.sfleadership.co.uk

Chapter 10: Strengths-focused meetings

1   Have a copy of the 10 features of strengths-focused meetings to hand at each team meeting:

    i   Start on a positive.

    ii Celebrate and explore successes.

    iii   Always have an outcome focus.

    iv   Focus on solution (as opposed to problem).

    v   Get from solution to action.

    vi   Get a good balance (between appreciation vs criticism, between asking others for ideas vs telling them yours, and between an inward focus within the team vs an outward focus beyond the team).

    vii Listen fully (without interruption).

    viii Take turns.

    ix   End on a positive note and acknowledge contributions.

    x   Evaluate:

        a   What was good about this meeting?

        b   How could we make it even better next time?

2 Use the strengths-focused version of the GROW model as an effective problem-solving, or solution-creating, tool.

3 Use ROW to review progress on previously set goals.

4 Follow the suggestions for actions before and after the meeting.

Chapter 11: Strengths-focused coaching

1 Create a regular diary slot for each member of your team. This will make coaching a regular habit and more strongly embed the tool and its behaviours.

2 Download our two coaching scripts (Strengths-Focused GROW and Progress Review Coaching) from our website at www.sfleadership. co.uk. Have these with you at each coaching session until you become so familiar with them that you don't need them any more.

Chapter 12: Strengths-focused performance appraisals

1 Take a look at your existing performance appraisal documentation. What opportunities do you have to introduce a strengths focus into your existing documents and processes?

2 Decide how you want to incorporate a strengths focus into your appraisals and do the necessary preparation: for example revising the documentation, 'strengthening' the structure of your conversation, becoming familiar with how to use the Five-Step Strengths Map.

3 Ensure your team members are clear about what the 'new' approach to appraisals will look like and what benefits they will get from focusing more on their strengths than their weaknesses.

4 Brief your team about how to prepare for their strengths-focused performance appraisal.

5 Use the 10 tips provided in this chapter to bring a strengths-focused approach to your appraisal discussions. Download the template of questions from our website at www.sfleadership.co.uk

6 Gather feedback from your team members about what they liked about the new approach to appraisal discussions. Ask them what suggestions they have for enhancing the process even further.

Chapter 13: Strengths-focused development discussions

1 Take a look at your existing processes for identifying development needs and writing development plans. How strengths-focused are the existing processes?

2 Determine what you need to do to introduce more of a strengths approach to your development conversations.

3 Download the templates on our website for some useful guidance on structure and content of strengths-focused development discussions.

4 Plan in time with each of your team members to either review existing development plans or construct new ones, ensuring that the emphasis is on developing strengths and addressing only significant weaknesses.

5 Practise having some strengths-focused development conversations and notice the results.

6 Review development plans regularly with your team members, emphasising what has been achieved.

Chapter 14: Strengths-focused recruitment

1 Take a look at your existing recruitment processes. How strengths-focused are they?

2 Determine what you need to do to introduce more of a strengths approach to your recruitment processes. Is this something you can do on your own, or do you need to enlist the help of your Human Resources team?

3 Download the templates on our website for some useful strengths-focused questions that you can use in the interview.

4 Liaise with your Human Resources team or those responsible for the organisation's recruitment processes and let them know what changes you would like to make.

5 Practise having some strengths-focused interviews and notice the results.

Chapter 15: High-performing teams

1 If they would be happy to do so, involve your team members in assessing how well the team has done each of the six steps.

2 For a more detailed assessment of the effectiveness of your team, visit our website at www.sfleadership.co.uk.

3 Involve your stakeholders in giving you 'team' feedback so that you have a more balanced external and internal view of your team's effectiveness.

4 To build higher performance in the team focus on each step sequentially, using our suggested activities.

5 Use all the suggestions of the book so far to 'strengthen' your team.

Chapter 16: Leading change

1 Follow our suggestions for:

    i   preparing yourself and your mindset;

    ii   launching a change project;

    iii progress reviews;

    iv ending a change project.

2 Build energy and involvement in the change by focusing on what's working and strengths. Use that energy and involvement to tackle what could be working better, as well as any significant weaknesses.

Chapter 17: Developing strategy

1 If developing strategy is your strength then play to it.

2 If developing strategy is not your strength, and is a significant weakness use our suggestions (in Chapter 4) to manage it. This could be about tapping into your other strengths or the strengths of others that relate to strategy, eg Creativity, Analytical Thinking, Strategic Thinking, Planner, Common Sense, Detail Focus, etc.

3 Use the assessment to highlight areas for action.

4 Follow our SPIRE process to build strategy around strengths.

On a final note

At the start of this book we maintained that you will be the best leader that you can be if you do the things that you are good at, that you love doing, and that give you great results. Strengths-focused leadership is about supporting those you lead to do the same.

This is the recipe for the ideal job and career as well as a recipe for business success.

We hope you are now clear about how to lead with a strengths focus. It's about understanding the mindset involved. It's about following the four steps of our MORE model, which are driven by that mindset and continue to strengthen it.

We also hope that this book is a useful toolbox that you can continually dip into as you develop your leadership style and as you approach the different activities of strengths-focused leadership.

Please feel free to access and download these tools from our website, and we recommend the video clips which demonstrate some of the key tools and processes that you may be unfamiliar with using.

We have found that a focus on what is best in people has enriched our lives not only at work but in life in general. So we wish you all those gifts that this approach can bring you.

www.sfleadership.co.uk

Appendix 1

Dictionary of strengths

A dictionary of strengths

THINKING STRENGTHS

Analytical Thinking Using logic, objectivity and critical thinking.

Common Sense Taking a practical, down-to-earth approach to thinking through challenges.

Creativity Coming up with new and innovative ideas.

Curiosity Interested to seek out new ideas, ways of thinking and facts.

Detail Focus Focusing on the specific facts and details in a situation.

Reflection Thinking things through in depth on one's own.

Strategic Thinking Focusing on the longer term, bigger picture view; seeing patterns and themes across current and future challenges.

EMOTIONAL STRENGTHS

Courage Taking on difficult and challenging situations.

Drive The motivation to push forward with challenges and goals.

Emotional Awareness Being aware in the now of one's own and other's emotions.

Emotional Balance Remaining calm in varied circumstances.

Enthusiasm Having energy and passion.

Optimism Seeing the best possibilities in any situation.

Persistence Sticking at it regardless of the challenges.

Resilience Handling continuous pressure in one's stride and bouncing back positively.

Self-confidence A strong belief in oneself and one's ability.

COMMUNICATING AND INFLUENCING STRENGTHS

Collaboration   Working well with others in joint endeavours.

Communicator   Communicating ideas effectively to others face to face. **Developer**   Developing others well.

Empathy   Recognising and appreciating the emotions of others.

Fairness   Treating every individual fairly.

Harmony   Creating harmony and positive feelings in others.

Humour   Generating humour and fun in a way that enables effective interactions.

Inclusion   Including others appropriately in a situation.

Leader   Stepping into a leadership role in situations.

Listener   Hearing the ideas, views and emotions of others in a way that ensures they feel listened to.

Motivator   Energising others towards a goal.

Persuasiveness   Convincing others towards a particular idea or way of seeing things.

Relationship Builder   Building new relationships.

Writer   Writing in a way that effectively communicates a message.

ACTION AND EXECUTION STRENGTHS

Adaptability   Changing plans quickly when needed to achieve results.

Decisiveness   Taking decisions in a timely manner, when needed.

Efficiency   Getting things done in the time frame.

Initiative   Stepping up and getting on with what is needed.

Organiser   Organising practicalities in complex situations.

Planner   Creating workable plans to achieve the desired results.

Problem Solver   Solving problems that stand in the way of the desired results.

Results Focus   Maintaining focus on the result required and staying headed in that direction.

Self-Improvement   Improving one's knowledge, skills and ways of thinking to improve results.

Appendix 2
Template for business objectives action plan

Objective	Measures of success	Strengths	Timing	Action plan
What is the objective?	How will you measure your achievement?	Which strengths are relevant to achieving this?	When is it to be achieved?	What actions will be taken to achieve the objective?

Appendix 3
Template for development objectives action plan

Development goal	Measures of success	Strengths	Action plan			Target date
			What are the specific actions I can take in support of each goal?			
What do I want to achieve and for what purpose?	How will each goal be measured?	Which strengths can I draw on to help me achieve this goal?	Work-related opportunities 70%	Others' support 20%	Formal training and self-directed learning activities 10%	

Appendix 4

A strengths-focused team development plan

Here is a development programme for a team that could be run across a period of approximately six months:

Month 1 (whole-day event):

▌ Give team members an overview of the six-month programme.

▌ Identify recent successes and challenges for the team.

▌ Clarify the team purpose and key goals both from an internal and external perspective.

▌ Following their one-to-one strengths debrief before the event, identify the individual and collective strengths in the team, and any important weaknesses.

▌ Identify actions to enhance the team's ability to play to its strengths.

Month 2 (half-day event):

▌ Identify the characteristics of a high-performing team.

▌ Clarify the results of a self-assessment by the team against a model of a high-performing team (e.g. six-step model described in Chapter 15).

▌ Analyse the strengths in the current performance of the team, any critical weaknesses, and identify areas for development.

▌ Identify behaviours for effective team work.

▌ Create a clear plan for enhancing team effectiveness.

▌ Identify a process for gaining stakeholder feedback on the team performance.

Month 3 (half-day event):

▌ Identify the results of stakeholder feedback on the performance of the team.

▌ Celebrate and analyse the strengths of the team identified by stakeholders and how this aligns with the team's internal perception of its strengths.

▌ Use a stakeholder mapping tool to analyse the current nature of stakeholder relationships.

▌ Identify desired 'Team Brand' – how the team wants to be perceived by its stakeholders.

▌ Identify the principles of effective influencing and relationship building.

▌ Create a plan to enhance existing stakeholder relationships.

Month 4 (half-day event):

▌ Celebrate and analyse actions and achievements taken since the previous event. What strengths were on show? Any significant weaknesses?

▌ Based on exploration at previous events, focus on key elements of team-working which have already progressed, and those that will further enhance the success of the team (e.g. communication, decision-making, problem-solving, conflict management, team meetings).

▌ Agree key actions ahead of final session.

Month 5 (half-day event):

▌ Celebrate and analyse actions and achievements taken since the previous event. What changes in team-working have been achieved? How have they incorporated individual strengths?

▌ Based on exploration at previous events, focus on key elements of team-working which have already progressed, and those that will further enhance the success of the team (e.g. communication, decision-making, problem-solving, conflict management, team meetings).

▌ Agree key actions ahead of final session, and how further diagnostics will be done.

Month 6 (half-day event):

▌ Celebrate and analyse achievements across the whole programme.

▌ Analyse results of a second team self-assessment (and stakeholder assessment).

▌ Highlight achievements in team-working across the programme.

▌ Clarify how the achievements will be built on, following the end of the current programme.

References

Adair, J. (1987) *Effective Team Building*, London, Pan Books.

Alexander, G. (2006) 'Behavioural Coaching: The GROW Model', in J. Passmore, ed., *Excellence in Coaching: The industry guide*, London, Kogan Page, pp. 61–72.

Arakawa, D. and Greenberg, M. (2007) 'Optimistic Managers and their Influence on Productivity and Employee Engagement in a Technology Organisation: Implications for coaching psychologists', *International Coaching Psychology Review* 2 (1), March 2007, pp. 78–112.

Bauer, T. N. (2010) *Onboarding New Employees: Maximizing success*, Alexandria, VA, SHRM Foundation.

Bolles, R. N. (2001) *What Color is your Parachute? A practical manual for job-hunters and career-changers*, Berkeley, CA, Ten Speed Press.

Buckingham, M. (2007) *Go Put your Strengths to Work*, London, Simon & Schuster UK Ltd.

Buckingham, M. and Coffman, C. (2005) *First Break All the Rules: What the world's greatest managers do differently*, London, Simon & Schuster.

Cable, D. M., et al. (2013) 'Reinventing Employee Onboarding', *MIT Sloan Management Review* Spring 2013, 19 March 2013.

Collins, J. (2001) *Good to Great: Why some companies make the leap . . . and others don't*, London, Random House.

Collins, J. (2006) *Good to Great and the Social Sectors: Why business thinking is not the answer*, Boulder, CO, Random House Business Books.

Cooperrider, D. L. and Srivastva, S. (1987) 'Appreciative Inquiry in Organizational Life', *Research in Organizational Change and Development* 1, pp. 129–69.

Corporate Leadership Council (2002) *Performance Management Survey*, Washington, DC.

Covey, S. R. (2004) *The 7 Habits of Highly Effective People*, New York, Simon & Schuster.

Csikszentmihalyi, M. (1990) *Flow: The psychology of optimal experience*, New York, Harper & Row.

De Shazer, S. (1985) *Keys to Solution in Brief Therapy*, New York, Norton.

De Shazer, S. Quoted in Berg, I. K. and Szabo, P. (2005) *Brief Coaching for Lasting Solutions*, London, W.W. Norton & Co., p. 1.

Drexler, A. B., Sibbet, D. and Forrester, R. H (1988) 'The Team Performance Model', in W. B. Reddy and K. Jamison (eds.) *Team Building: Blueprints for Productivity and Satisfaction*, Alexandria, Virginia and San Diego: NTL Institute for Applied Behavioral Science and University Associates, Inc., pp. 45–62.

Drucker, P. F. (1967) *The Effective Executive*, London, Heinemann.

Drucker, P. F. Quoted in Buckingham, M. and Clifton, D. O. (2001) *Now, Discover your Strengths: How to develop your talents and those of the people you manage*, London, Simon & Schuster.

Fielden, D. S. (2005). *Literature Review: Coaching effectiveness – a summary. A summary of a report for the NHS Leadership Centre by Dr Sandra Fielden of Centre for Diversity and Work Psychology*, Manchester Business School, University of Manchester. Research into Leadership, Modernisation Agency Leadership Centre.

Fredrickson, B. (2001) 'The Role of Positive Emotions in Positive Psychology: The broaden-and-build theory of positive emotions', *American Psychologist* 56 (3), pp. 218–26.

Goldsmith, M. *FeedForward*. www.marshallgoldsmithfeedforward.com Accessed 21.7.14.

Govindji, R. and Linley, A. (2007) 'Strengths Use, Self-Concordance and Well-Being: Implications for strengths coaching and coaching psychologists', *International Coaching Psychology Review* 2 (2), pp. 143–53.

Grant, A. M. (2012) 'Making Positive Change: A randomized study comparing solution-focused vs. problem-focused coaching questions', *Journal of Systemic Therapies* 31 (2), pp. 21–35.

Hackman, J. R. (1987) 'The Design of Work Teams', in J. Lorsch (ed.), *Handbook of Organizational Behaviour*, New York, Prentice-Hall, pp. 315–42.

Hackman, J. R. (2002) *Leading Teams: Setting the stage for great performances*, Boston, MA., Harvard Business School Press.

Haldane, B. (1947) 'A Pattern for Executive Placement', *Harvard Business Review* 25 (4a), pp. 652–63.

Harter, J. K., et al. (2002) 'Business-Unit-Level Relationship between Employee Satisfaction, Employee Engagement, and Business Outcomes: A meta-analysis', *Journal of Applied Psychology* 87 (2) (April 2002), pp. 268–79.

Hawkins, P. (2011) *Leadership Team Coaching: Developing collective transformational leadership*, London, Kogan Page.

Isern, J. and Pung, C. (2006) 'Organizing for Successful Change Management: A McKinsey global survey', *The McKinsey Quarterly*, June 2006.

Jackson, P. and McKergow, M. (2002) *The Solutions Focus: The SIMPLE way to positive change*, London, Nicholas Brealey Publishing.

Jones, D. (2001) 'Celebrate What's Right With the World', available at www.celebratewhatsright.com Accessed 21.7.14.

Katzenbach, J. R. and Smith, D. K. (1993) *The Wisdom of Teams: Creating the high-performance organization*, Boston, MA, Harvard Business School Press.

Keller, S. and Price, C. (2011) *Beyond Performance: How great organizations build ultimate competitive advantage*, Hoboken, NJ, Wiley.

Kline, N. (1999) *Time to Think: Listening to ignite the human mind*, London, Ward Lock.

Kotter, J. P. (1996) *Leading Change*, Boston, MA, Harvard Business School Press.

Kouzes, J. M. and Posner, B. Z. (2002) *The Leadership Challenge* (3rd edn), San Francisco, Jossey-Bass.

Linley, A. (2008) *Average to A+: Realising strengths in yourself and others*, Coventry, CAPP Press.

Linley, A. P., et al. (2010) 'Using Signature Strengths in Pursuit of Goals: Effects on goal progress, need satisfaction, and well-being, and implications for coaching psychologists', *International Coaching Psychology Review* 5 (1), pp. 6–15.

Linley, A., Willars, J. and Biswas-Diener, R. (2010) *The Strengths Book: Be confident, be successful, and enjoy better relationships by realising the best in you*, Coventry, CAPP Press.

Lombardo, M. M. and Eichinger, R. W. (1996) *The Career Architect Development Planner* (1st edn), Minneapolis, Lominger.

Losada, M. and Heaphy, E. (2004) 'The Role of Positivity and Connectivity in the Performance of Business Teams: A nonlinear dynamics model', *American Behavioral Scientist* 47, pp. 740–65.

McKinsey and Company (2010) *What Successful Transformations Share: McKinsey Global Survey results.* www.mckinsey.com/insights/organization/what_successful_transformations_share_mckinsey_global_survey_results Accessed 21.7.14.

Michie, S. and Williams, S. (2003) 'Reducing Work Related Psychological Ill Health and Sickness Absence: A systematic literature review', *Occupational & Environmental Medicine* (60), pp. 3–9.

NICE (The National Institute for Health & Clinical Excellence) (2007) *Behaviour Change: NICE public health guidance 6.* www.nice.org.uk/guidance/ph6/resources/guidance-behaviour-change-the-principles-for-effective-interventions-pdf. Accessed 21.7.14.

Peters, T. J. and Waterman, R. H. (1982) *In Search of Excellence: Lessons from America's best-run companies*, New York, Harper & Row.

Peterson, C. and Seligman, M. E. P. (2004) *Character Strengths and Virtues: A handbook and classification*, Washington, DC, American Psychological Association.

Proctor, C., Maltby, J. and Linley, A. (2009) 'Strengths Use as a Predictor of Well Being and Health-Related Quality of Life', *Journal of Happiness Studies* 12 (1), 153–69.

Rapp, C. A. (1998) *The Strengths Model: Case management with people suffering from severe and persistent mental illness*, New York & Oxford, Oxford University Press.

Rath, T. (2007) *Strengths Finder 2.0*, New York, Gallup Press.

Rath, T. and Conchie, B. (2008) *Strengths Based Leadership: Great leaders, teams, and why people follow*, New York, Gallup Press.

Repper, J. and Perkins, R. (2003) *Social Inclusion and Recovery: A model for mental health practice*, Edinburgh, Bailliere Tindall.

Rollag, K., Parise, S., and Cross, R. (2005) 'Getting New Hires Up to Speed Quickly', *MIT Sloan Management Review* 46, pp. 35–41.

Rozin, P. and Royzman, E. B. (2001) 'Negativity Bias, Negativity Dominance, and Contagion', *Personality and Social Psychology Review* 5 (4), pp. 296–320.

Saleebey, D. (2012). *The Strengths Perspective in Social Work Practice*, London, Pearson Education.

Schwartz, R. M. (2013) *Smart Leaders, Smart Teams: How you and your team get unstuck to get results*, San Francisco, Jossey-Bass.

Seligman, M. and Csikszentmihalyi, M. (2000) 'Positive Psychology: An introduction', *American Psychologist* 55 (1), pp. 5–14.

Smart, B. (1999) *Topgrading: How leading companies win by hiring, coaching, and keeping the best people*, Upper Saddle River, NJ: Prentice Hall.

Sundstrom, E., De Meuse, K. and Futtrell, D. (1990) 'Work Teams: Applications and effectiveness', *American Psychologist* 45 (2), pp. 120–33.

Toogood, K. (2012) 'Strengthening Coaching: An exploration of the mindset of executive coaches using strengths-based coaching', *International Journal of Evidence Based Coaching & Mentoring* (Special Issue No. 6), pp. 72–87.

Wagner, R. and Harter, J. K. (2006) *The 12 Elements of Great Managing*, New York, Gallup Press.

Watkins, M. (2013) *The First 90 Days, Updated and Expanded: Critical success strategies for new leaders at all levels*, Boston, MA., Harvard Business School Press.

Wood, A., et al. (2011) 'Using Personal and Psychological Strengths Leads to Increases in Well-Being over Time: A longitudinal study and the development of strengths use questionnaire', *Personality and Individual Differences* 50 (1), pp. 15–19.

Zenger, J. H. and Folkman, J. (2009) *The Extraordinary Leader: Turning good managers into great leaders*, New York, McGraw-Hill Professional.

Zenger, J. H., et al. (2012) *How to be Exceptional: Drive leadership success by magnifying your strengths*, New York, McGraw-Hill.

Index

Written by the CEO of the CMI, this authoritative guide to management provides engaging and practical information on every element of managing people, processes and resources.

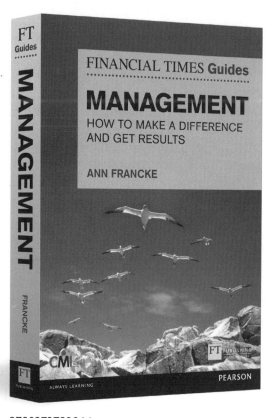

FT Guides

MANAGEMENT

FRANCKE

FINANCIAL TIMES Guides

MANAGEMENT

HOW TO MAKE A DIFFERENCE AND GET RESULTS

ANN FRANCKE

CMI

FT PUBLISHING

PEARSON

ALWAYS LEARNING

FT PUBLISHING

9780273792864

"Practical, concise and full of tips every manager needs to know, it provides a powerful guide for leaders at every level."
– Arianna Huffington, Chairman, President, and Editor-in-Chief of the Huffington Post Media Group

"Amidst the myriad of books on leadership, this guide presents an unusually concrete, comprehensive and practical set of principles and learnings for managers at every level."
– John Pepper, Former CEO & Chairman P&G; Former Chairman Walt Disney

"This is clear, encouraging and packed with good sense - just like its author. A winner."
– Eleanor Mills, Editorial Director, The Sunday Times

Whether you're a new team leader or an experienced director, this book contains everything you need to know to become an outstanding manager.

Available from all good bookshops

FT PUBLISHING
FINANCIAL TIMES